An Islamic Alliance

Northwestern University Press

Series in Islam and Society in Africa

An Islamic Alliance *'Alī Dīnār and the Sānūsiyya, 1906–1916*

JAY SPAULDING and LIDWIEN KAPTEIJNS

Northwestern University Press
EVANSTON, ILLINOIS
1994

Northwestern University Press
www.nupress.northwestern.edu

10 9 8 7 6 5 4 3 2 1

ISBN 978-0-8101-2809-5

The Library of Congress has cataloged the original, hardcover edition as follows:

An Islamic alliance : 'Alī Dīnār and the Sānūsiyya, 1906–1916 / Jay Spaulding and Lidwien Kapteijns.
p. cm. — (Series in Islam and society in Africa)
Chiefly documents in Arabic with English translations and notes.
Includes bibliographical references (p.) and index.
ISBN 0-8101-1194-2
1. Darfur (Sudan)—History—Sources. 2. Wadai (Sultanate—History—Sources. 3. 'Alī Dīnār, Sultan of Darfur, d. 1916. 4. Senussites—Chad—Wadai (Sultanate)—History—Sources. I. Spaulding, Jay. II. Kapteijns, Lidwien. III. Series.
DT159.6.D2&I85 1994
962.7—dc20 94-31895
CIP

∞The paper used in this publication meets the minimum requirements of the American National Standard for Information Sciences—Permanence of Paper for Printed Library Materials, ANSI Z39.48-1992.

This book is respectfully dedicated to the memory of

ʿAlī Dīnār b. Zakariyāʾ

Aḥmad al-Sharīf al-Sanūsī

CONTENTS

ACKNOWLEDGEMENTS

We gratefully acknowledge Dr. Muḥammad Ibrāhīm Abū Salīm, Director of the National Records Office, Khartoum, for permission to publish the texts of the documents offered here. We are grateful to the Departments of History at Wellesley College and at Kean College of New Jersey for institutional support. Aḥmad al-`Awaḍ Sikainga and Mohamed Daahir Afrah have advised us in regard to several idiomatic and orthographic questions, and G.M. LaRue kindly shared some of his archival notes.

NOTE ON TRANSLITERATION

Arabic words have been transliterated according to the Middle East Times system. We have not aimed at complete consistency in regard to place names; a few comparatively familiar sites (Benghazi, El Obeid) follow informal western cartographic convention, but most (al-Fāshir, al-Nahūd) have been transliterated as Arabic words.

INTRODUCTION

This volume is a contribution to the growing literature of documentary source publications from northeastern Africa.[1] Its primary purpose is to help restore African voices to an historiography too often dominated by the perceptions of Europeans, and to allow authentically African definitions of historical experience to emerge. The authors offer no apology for the fact that the work consists of an incomplete and historically scattered collection of "textual fragments,"[2] but they do invite the reader to reflect carefully and critically upon the architecture of interpretation advanced here to lend a structure of meaning to a damaged record; clearly, what is offered is merely a small part of a much larger discourse.

---

[1]Glauco Ciammaichella, *Libyens et Français au Tchad (1897-1914): La confrérie Senoussie et le commerce transsaharien.* Paris: CNRS, 1987; Aḥmad Ṣidqī al-Dajjānī, *al-Ḥaraka al-Sanūsiyya: nasha'atuhā wa-numūwuhā fī'l-qarn al-tāsi` `ashar.* Beirut: Dār Lubnān, 1967; Lidwien Kapteijns and Jay Spaulding, *After the Millennium: Diplomatic Correspondence from Wadai and Dār Fūr on the Eve of Colonial Conquest, 1885-1916.* East Lansing: African Studies Center, Michigan State University, 1988; Helmut Klopfer, *Aspekte der Bewegung des Muḥammad Ben `Alī as-Sanūsī.* Wiesbaden: Otto Harrassowitz, 1967; R.S. O'Fahey and M.I. Abū Salīm, *Land in Dār Fūr: Charters and related documents from the Dār Fūr Sultanate.* Cambridge: Cambridge University Press, 1983; and Jean-Louis Triaud, *Tchad 1900-1902: Une Guerre Franco-Libyenne Oubliée? Une confrérie musulmane, La Sanūsiyya face à la France.* Paris: Harmattan, 1987. See also two dissertations: Knut S. Vikör, "Saint and Scholar on the Desert Edge: Muḥammad b. `Alī al-Sanūsi (1787-1859)," University of Bergen, 1991 and Jean-Louis Triaud, "Les Relations entre la France et la Sanûsiyya (1840-1930): Histoire d'une mythologie coloniale, Découverte d'une confrérie saharienne," University of Paris, 1991.

[2]Edward W. Said, *Orientalism* (New York: Random House, 1978), p. 128.

The subject of this book is the defense, by devoutly Islamic leaders, of one of the last parts of the African continent to be overrun by the imperial European "Scramble for Africa" during the decade that culminated in the First World War, a region which extended south from the Mediterranean coast of Cyrenaica for more than two thousand miles to embrace parts of northern Chad, and the sultanate of Dār Fūr in the western portion of the modern Republic of the Sudan.

The defense of an embattled African *Dār al-Islām* is the theme that unifies the documents presented here, thirty fortuitously surviving pieces of diplomatic correspondence between `Alī Dīnār, the prince who restored an independent Dār Fūr, and the contemporary leaders of the Sanūsī brotherhood, based from 1902 in the southern Libyan oasis of Kufra.[3] In contrast to a prevailing historiography which asserts that cooperation between `Alī Dīnār and the Sanūsiyya was no more than an ephemeral dream or a "crazy plan," the present sources seem rather to indicate that there existed a real, passionately felt alliance, balanced in reciprocity according to changing historical vicissitudes.[4] In

[3]Nicola A. Ziadeh, *Sanūsīyah: A Study of a Revivalist Movement in Islam*, 2nd ed. (Leiden: Brill, 1983), p. 66; E.E. Evans-Pritchard, *The Sanusi of Cyrenaica* (Oxford: Clarendon Press, 1949), p. 27.

[4]The presently dominant viewpoint was expressed well by Evans-Pritchard: "It is often said by writers, and the view seems to have been held by British Intelligence, though I do not know on what evidence, that he [Aḥmad al-Sharīf] intended to link up with a revolt (November 1915) of `Ali Dinar, the Sultan of Darfur in the Egyptian Sudan, though the Sultan had never been friendly towards the Sanusiya. It is quite possible that the Turks or the Sayyid, or both, had some such crazy plan." (*The Sanusi*, p. 128). The attitude of Anglo-Egyptian intelligence was summarized by A.B. Theobald: "The resources of the Sanūsiya themselves were, however, so slender, the distances involved so vast, and the carrying capacity of a train of camels across a barren desert so small, that such reinforcements from the Sanūsiya could only be a gesture of support, and never a factor of any real significance." (*`Alī Dīnār, Last Sultan of Darfur, 1898-1916* [London: Longmans, 1965], p. 163). The possibility that `Alī Dīnār might have made significant contributions to the success of the Sanūsiyya has not been considered. See also Triaud, "Relations," pp. 844-846.

practice, to be sure, the tangible qualities of this alliance were conditioned and limited not only by the difficulties of communication, transport and political control across vast distances and extremely austere terrain, but also by the distinctly differing sets of social expectations and political assumptions held by a conservative African monarch grounded in the ancient tradition of Sudanic kingship and the managers of a modern, transcontinental, polyethnic sociopolitical organization that certainly encouraged and perhaps to some extent depended upon the practice of commerce by private individuals.[5]

The first part of the study to follow is an extended interpretive essay, organized chronologically, that attempts to place the documents themselves and the information they contain in a wider historical context. At the first mention of people and places that appear in the present collection of documents, each name will be marked with an asterisk. The second part presents the documents themselves, with English translations and notes originating from the process of reading and translating. Words left untranslated appear in italics and, if not explained in a footnote, are entered in the glossary.

* * *

The Mahdist state in the Sudan fell to Anglo-Egyptian invaders at Karari on 2 September 1898.[6] Turning his back on the battlefield near the Mahdist capital of Omdurman, `Alī Dīnār b. Zakariyā'* of Dār Fūr,* one of the princely

[5]For Sanūsī commercial activities see Dennis D. Cordell, "Eastern Libya, Wadai and the Sanūsiya: A *Ṭarīqa* and a Trade Route," *Journal of African History* XVIII, 1 (1977), 21-36 and the sources cited in note 1 above. For the administered economy and commerce of northeast African kingdoms, see Lidwien Kapteijns, "The Organization of Exchange in Precolonial Western Sudan," in Leif O. Manger, ed., *Trade and Traders in the Sudan* (Bergen: Institute of Social Anthropology, University of Bergen, 1984), pp. 49-80 and Lidwien Kapteijns and Jay Spaulding, "Pre-Colonial Trade Between States in the Eastern Sudan, c. 1700 - c.1900," in Norman O'Neill and Jay O'Brien, eds., *Economy and Class in Sudan* (Aldershot: Avebury, 1988), pp. 60-89.

[6]`Ismat Hasan Zulfo, *Karari: The Sudanese Account of the Battle of Omdurman*, trans. Peter Clark. London: Frederick Warne, 1980.

hostages from the outlying provinces summoned to service and held for years under military discipline by the Khalīfa `Abdullāhi, now abandoned the Nile valley to its new foreign conquerors and rode west to claim the ancestral throne of his grandfather, Sultan Muḥammad al-Faḍl.*[7] During the next three years 'Alī Dīnār struck down rival contenders to the throne of Dār Fūr, rendered harmless most of the surviving Mahdist agents in the area, and reasserted his authority over many of the core groups of commoners who had traditionally been subject to the sultanate of Dār Fūr. He also launched a series of vigorous diplomatic initiatives among outlying communities whose historical ties to Dār Fūr were more equivocal; his missions were soon being received from Dār Sila in the west to Dār Kuti in the south and Taqalī in the east; the new monarch 's self-defined sphere of influence thus extended from the Nuba Mountains and the White Nile into Chad and the modern Central African Republic.[8] By the waning of the year 1901 `Alī Dīnār's eastward initiatives had drawn a response from the new masters in the Nile valley; in November Anglo-Egyptian forces were sent west to stem further Dār Fūr intervention in Kordofan, while `Alī Dīnār himself was instructed to accommodate himself to his assigned role as a client of the new British-dominated colonial regime.

As the nineteenth century drew to a close the Sanūsī brotherhood* stood at the height of its spiritual and temporal power. In 1899 Sayyid Muḥammad al-Mahdī,* son and worthy successor to the eminent founder of the order, moved the headquarters of the organization south out of Libya to the rocky oasis of Gouro (Qīrū)* near the eastern edge of the highlands of Tibesti in northern Chad.[9] It was said that al-Mahdī came to Gouro with his two young sons,[10]

[7]For an outline of the sultan's biography, see Theobald, *'Alī Dīnār*.

[8]Lidwien Kapteijns and Jay Spaulding, "Gifts Worthy of Kings: An Episode in Dār Fūr - Taqali Relations," *Sudanic Africa* 1 (1990), 61-70; and *After the Millennium*, Docs. 70-76, pp. 350-379 and Docs. 87-118, pp. 438-566.

[9]See Document 21 and Triaud, *Tchad*, p. 135 and Plate XVIII.

[10]Triaud, *Tchad*, p. 40.

[11]Documents 4, 14 and 18.

[12]Documents 4, 14, 18, 22, 26 and 29.

Muḥammad al-Riḍā*[11] and Muḥammad Idrīs.*[12] Of particular immediate importance for the next generation of Sanūsī leadership, however, were the several sons of al-Mahdī's late brother, Sayyid Muḥammad al-Sharīf; these included Aḥmad al-Sharīf*[13] and Muḥammad `Ābid,*[14] both of whom were old enough at the time to have begun participating in public affairs.[15] A day of eminence would also come soon for their younger brothers `Alī al-Khaṭṭābī,*[16] Muḥammad Hilāl*[17] and Muḥammad Ṣafī al-Dīn.*[18] Another supporter of al-Mahdī at Gouro, who perhaps stood as close to him as any kinsman, was the elderly Sayyid Aḥmad al-Rifī,* a survivor out of the previous generation, highly honored as one of the early companions of the Grand Sanūsī (Muḥammad b. `Alī) himself.[19]

Among the concerns that brought al-Mahdī south to Gouro in 1899 was a sense of responsibility toward the rapidly expanding sphere of Sanūsī influence in the central Sahara and beyond. Earlier in the same year an important new frontier outpost had been founded far to the southwest near the shores of Lake Chad at Bir Alali, as a forward base for proselytizing among the rulers and subjects of the region.[20] The new mission field attracted some of the best Sanūsī agents. Ibrāhīm al-Gharbī,*[21] for example, arrived at Bir Alali with impeccable academic credentials in the form of a letter of recommendation from Gouro: "Si vous trouvez un endroit pour lui où il puisse professer," Aḥmad al-Rifī advised Sīdī al-Barrānī, the head of the new southwestern settlement, "installez-le et recommandez-le."[22] During 1901 Ibrāhīm al-Gharbī with two

13Documents 4, 10, 13, 14, 20, 22, 23, 26, 27 and 30.

14Documents 2, 3, 4, 6, 7, 8, 12, 14, 15, 16, 22, 25, 26, 27 and 30.

15Triaud, *Tchad*, Docs. 4, 10 and 28.

16Documents 5 and 17.

17Document 20.

18Document 27.

19Documents 9, 13, 14, 16, 20 and 22; Triaud, *Tchad*, Docs. 8, 11, 14, 21 and 22.

20For an introduction to the *zāwiya* of Bir Alali, see Triaud, *Tchad*, pp. 11-36.

21Documents 10 and 12.

22Triaud, *Tchad*, pp. 110-112 and Plate VIII.

companions made a missionary journey to the people of the islands of Lake Chad; as a result, they began sending welcome supplies of food to Bir Alali.[23]

The southward expansion of the Sanūsiyya was also an economic movement fueled by the opportunity for commercial profit through the importation into outposts such as Bir Alali of trade goods available at the Mediterranean coast, notably fabrics, tea, sugar, firearms and ammunition, and the export north of slaves, ivory, livestock and other African products.[24] Foremost among the merchants of Sanūsī loyalty were the Majābra,*[25] inhabitants of the Cyrenaican oasis of Jalo: "the desert is a sea," as one of them put it, "and Jalo is its port."[26] When the Sanūsiyya adopted Kufra*[27] as headquarters, first in 1895 and again after 1902, merchants and caravaneers from among its chief inhabitants, the Zuwayya,*[28] rose to new prominence within the Sanūsī trading community. But the Sanūsī merchants were a cosmopolitan group; represented in the present collection of documents are traders from the Fazzān,*[29] from the Magharba of the Sirtican coast,[30] from Ghadames,*[31] from the Bū Ḥalayqa* family of the coastal Cyrenaican Hasa,[32] and very likely others. Considered as a merchant diaspora distributed between oasis settlements through lands held by stateless societies, the axis of Sanūsī free commercial activities extended from the Sirtica to Lake Chad down a

[23]Triaud, *Tchad*, pp. 111-112, note 1.

[24]For economically-grounded perspectives see Ciammaichella, *Libyens et Français*; Cordell, "Eastern Libya," and Steven Baier, "Trans-Saharan Trade and the Sahel: Damergu, 1870-1930," *Journal of African History* XVIII, 1 (1977), 37-60.

[25]Documents 4, 13, 24, 26 and 29.

[26]A.M. Hassanein, *The Lost Oases* (New York: Century, 1925), p. 88.

[27]Documents 13, 15, 22, 24, 26 and 29.

[28]Documents 9, 28 and 29.

[29]Documents 27 and 29.

[30]Document 25.

[31]Documents 2, 4, 7, 13, 19, 26 and 29.

[32]Documents 15 and 25.

corridor of Libyan influence already pioneered over the preceding century by the southward dispersal of the Awlād Sulaymān.*[33]

Conspicuously absent from the ranks of the Sanūsī merchant community as they appear in the present collection of documents were citizens of the kingdoms of the eastern Sudan affiliated with the order; foremost of these was Wadai,* whose sultan Muḥammad Sharīf (1834-1858) had been converted as a young prince by the Grand Sanūsī himself, and which remained consistently loyal to the Sanūsiyya thereafter.[34] From the perspective of the sultans of Wadai or Dār Fūr, or of the small buffer states that defended a precarious autonomy between these two large regional powers, a country's import-export trade should be administered by the ruler; the participation of subjects in commerce was limited to certain restricted and comparatively modest spheres of exchange, while foreign merchants, conceivably men of Sanūsī loyalties, might indeed be invited to enter a kingdom such as Wadai, but only under substantial royal constraints on what they would otherwise have regarded as normal business practice.[35]

The interaction of the fundamentally different systems of exchange conceived and practiced by private merchants and Sudanese kings provided many opportunities for misunderstanding and conflict of interest. Sometimes the clash of principles and practice pitted foreign merchants against their royal hosts; for example, Document 19 expresses eloquently the discontent felt by private merchants obliged to hand over their wares (including presents intended for another monarch) to the sultan of Dār Tāmā, in return for which they were compelled to accept in payment such goods as the king saw fit to give them at such a time--long delayed--as seemed convenient to him.[36] In other cases tension developed between the court, with the community of foreign merchants it patronized, and the subjects of the kingdom, who resented their own exclusion from this form of prosperity and the royal display of favoritism

[33]Document 22. Some historical background may be found in Gustav Nachtigal, *Sahara and Sudan II: Kawar, Bornu, Kanem, Borku, Ennedi,* trans. Allan G.B. Fisher and Humphrey J. Fisher (London: Hurst, 1980), pp. 308-318.

[34]Ziadeh, *Sanūsīya*, pp. 49-50; Evans-Pritchard, *The Sanusi*, p. 16.

[35]See Kapteijns, "Organization of Exchange," Kapteijns and Spaulding, "Pre-Colonial Trade" and *After the Millennium*, pp. 22-25.

[36]Document 19; in this case a colonial governor provided redress.

toward privileged foreigners. This problem was conspicuous in Wadai when Gustav Nachtigal visited the capital of Sultan `Alī (1858-1974):

> The higher the esteem in which the king with his partiality for trade and commerce held the foreign merchants, and the greater the profit gained by them from their activities in the country, the more unpopular they were with the natives. With their boundless fear of the king, the natives indeed tolerated the foreigners, but nevertheless looked on them as intruders and parasites who lived sumptuously at their expense.[37]

Questions about economic policy and the status of resident foreigners often became contentious issues within the body politic, to the extent that controversy over the merits of commercial *infitāḥ* might well influence the fate of monarchs and the conduct of foreign relations.

The challenge to royal concepts of political economy in African "states without cities"[38] posed by private merchants committed to Mediterranean commercial usages antedated the rise of the Sanūsiyya and was by no means confined to relations between that organization and its affiliated kings.[39] However, the controversial role played by any foreign private trader in a "state without cities" did dampen the enthusiasm of such kings for accepting within their borders the presence of the archtypical, and elsewhere ubiquitous, Sanūsī local institution, the *zāwiya**--these communities constituting "véritables centres urbains où s'organisent les études, l'accueil des commerçants et des courriers, et la mise en exploitation par les esclaves des terres cultivables environnantes."[40]

It is against this background that one may comprehend the otherwise peculiar tradition attributed by the Sanūsī themselves in later years to Sultan

[37]Gustav Nachtigal, *Sahara and Sudan IV: Wadai and Darfur*, trans. Allan G.B. Fisher and Humphrey Fisher (Berkeley and Los Angeles: University of California Press, 1971), p. 57.

[38]For the importance of this key concept, see Lidwien Kapteijns and Jay Spaulding, *Een Kennismaking met de Afrikaanse Geschiedenis* (Muiderberg: Coutinho, 1985), pp. 47-75.

[39]For examples from the Nile valley see Jay Spaulding, "The Management of Exchange in Sinnār, c. 1700," in Manger, *Trade and Traders*, pp. 25-48, and *The Heroic Age in Sinnār* (East Lansing: African Studies Center, Michigan State University, 1985), Part II, pp. 139-296.

[40]Triaud, *Tchad*, pp. 16-17; see also Ziadeh, *Sanūsīya*, pp. 104-116.

Muḥammad Sharīf, the first ruler of Wadai to embrace the order. "We will always be your friends and allies," the young king was said to have told his new spiritual master the Grand Sanūsī, "but if you build a zawiya here [in Wadai] the next thing you do will be to come and conquer us!"[41] Muḥammad Sharīf was as good as his word; no *zāwiya* was built in his days, and indeed his reign was noteworthy for his concerted attempt to rid his country of all foreign merchants, Sanūsī or otherwise.[42] The kings who followed Muḥammad Sharīf on the throne of Wadai, however, adopted a much more relaxed attitude, and by the end of the century Wadai had become an important participant in the far-flung central Saharan trading diaspora of Sanūsī loyalties.[43] Several Sanūsī *zāwiyas* were built in Wadai,[44] and the staff of the one situated in the merchants' enclave adjoining the capital was said to number about five hundred.[45] It included many eminent Sanūsī individuals under the leadership of Muḥammad al-Sunnī; not least among these was the prominent trader and diplomat Abū Bakr al-Ghadāmsī,* soon to play an important role in Dār Fūr-Sanūsiyya relations.[46]

As 'Alī Dīnār began his quest to restore the Dār Fūr sultanate at the close of 1898, the Sanūsī brotherhood was nearing the apogee of its spiritual eminence and temporal influence. While the evidence concerning 'Alī Dīnār's earliest relations with the Sanūsiyya is imperfect and often indirect, the sources available do seem to indicate that during the earliest years of his reign the new sultan of Dār Fūr sought to establish a friendly accomodation with the order. According to Sanūsī tradition, during 'Alī Dīnār's first year in power, (while Sayyid al-Mahdī was still in Kufra preparing for the transfer of the seat of the order to Gouro in August 1899), the young king sent to Kufra "a deputation . . .

[41]Rosita Forbes, *The Secret of the Sahara: Kufara* (New York: Cassell, 1921), p. 119. Forbes' informant was 'Abd al-Raḥīm, commander of the escort of military slaves assigned to guard her by Muḥammad al-Riḍā.

[42]Nachtigal, *Sahara and Sudan IV: Wadai and Darfur*, pp. 51, 57.

[43]For a discussion, see Cordell, "Eastern Libya."

[44]Existing attempts to list all Sanūsī *zāwiyas* do not inspire complete confidence; see Ziadeh, *Sanūsīya*, pp. 99-104 and Evans-Pritchard, *The Sanusi*, p. 24.

[45]Khartoum, Sudan; National Records Office (hereafter, NRO) Intelligence 2/15/125.

[46]Ibid.; Documents 2, 4, 7, 13, 19, 26 and 29.

expressing the Sultan of Dar Fur's devotion to the order."[47] The Anglo-Egyptian spy Ṣāliḥ Jibrīl, who visited al-Fāshir during 1900, reported that `Alī Dīnār was referring publicly to al-Mahdī as "our lord," and asserting that all the free kings west of the Nile "were in accord with El Senussi."[48] Other intelligence sources indicated that `Alī Dīnār had sent "presents" to the Sanūsiyya, perhaps best exemplified by the consignment register offered here in Document 1. This act had greater significance than the European spymasters on the Nile may have realized, for as Jean-Louis Triaud has noted, "la circulation des cadeaux constituait une des grandes sources de revenus--peut-être la principale--pour la direction du mouvement."[49] In return, during the first half of 1901 `Alī Dīnār received Sanūsī banners and devotional literature.[50]

These documented contacts between `Alī Dīnār and the Sanūsiyya certainly implied the coming and going of messengers and agents--perhaps many of them--and it seems fair to infer that under these circumstances there must have arisen the question of to what extent Dār Fūr, like its western neighbor Wadai, would be opened to Sanūsī traders and Sanūsī missionaries. Anglo-Egyptian intelligence was confident that `Alī Dīnār, like his Wadaian predecessor Sultan Muḥammad Sharif, would make "various excuses against any project for the establishment of a 'zawia' in Darfur...The fact undoubtedly was that Ali Dinar saw northern Wadai deeply influenced by the Senussi's power and had no intention of allowing his own authority to be made less absolute by the introduction of such a powerful factor."[51] The present authors believe that `Alī Dīnār was indeed reluctant to make concessions to the Sanūsiyya comparable to those granted by the Wadaian sultans of the later nineteenth century. However, there is also evidence that during the early years of `Alī Dīnār's reign, while both his own position within Dār Fūr and the role of Dār Fūr as a major regional power with very widespread imperial pretensions remained unclarified, the young king was unwilling to deny the wishes of the eminent master of Gouro;

[47]Forbes, *Kufara*, p. 327.

[48]NRO Darfur 1/3/16 and NRO Darfur 1/33/170.

[49]Triaud, *Tchad*, p. 69.

[50]NRO Darfur 1/3/16.

[51]Ibid. See also Triaud, "Relations," pp. 844-846.

points yielded at al-Fāshir could be balanced by the grant of privileges in other parts of the vast sphere of Sanūsī influence. For example, Anglo-Egyptian authorities on the Nile in 1901 speculated that `Alī Dīnār's diplomatic offensive eastward into Kordofan during that period expressed his confidence in Sanūsī backing.[52]

One common idiom in which the question of the admission of outsiders to a Sudanic kingdom was expressed was that of "opening of a road" to foreigners and foreign trade.[53] `Alī Dīnār, during his first years in power, was confronted with a call for "opening a road" in one of the most dramatic forms conceivable, for no sooner had Sayyid al-Mahdī accomplished the move of his headquarters from Kufra to Gouro than the Sanūsī leader, advanced in years and perhaps failing in health, in 1900 began to plan the culmination of his career with a pilgrimage to Mecca by way of Dār Fūr. One may doubt that `Alī Dīnār would have cherished the prospect of the Sayyid's procession through his land with a large retinue,[54] but he did not deny him passage, and in July 1900 duly notified the Anglo-Egyptian authorities of the route al-Mahdī intended to follow after passing east beyond the borders of Dār Fūr.[55] Preparatory arrangements for the Sayyid's anticipated pilgrimage continued for several years, and ended only with al-Mahdī's death at Gouro on 24 Ṣafar 1320/2 June 1902.

Meanwhile `Alī Dīnār, while preparing to open his country to one of the most eminent Islamic leaders of his day, could hardly exclude that leader's subordinates. For several years members of the Sanūsī trading diaspora passed through northern Dār Fūr on their wider journeys, were admitted to the capital, and may also have been allowed into other parts of the kingdom. Finally, it would seem that Sayyid al-Mahdī did indeed prevail upon `Alī Dīnār to accept the establishment of one or more Sanūsī *zāwiyas* in Dar Fūr.[56] Sayyid al-Mahdī

[52]NRO Darfur 1/3/16.

[53]Documents 13, 24, 28 and 29.

[54]Theobald, for example (*`Alī Dīnār*, pp. 58-59) believed that "`Alī Dīnār replied that his country was too poor to support the Sanūsī and his large party."

[55]Letter of 9 Rabī` I 1318/7 July 1900; NRO Intelligence 2/3/14.

[56]See Triaud, "Relations," p. 845 and Cordell, "Eastern Libya," p. 33; his sources, however, which place Jabal Marra in Wadai, do not inspire complete confidence.

delegated the task of founding the first Dār Fūr *zāwiya* to the head of the large Sanūsī establishment at the capital of Wadai; he in turn sent to al-Fāshir the prominent trader Aḥmad al-Tuwāṭī, accompanied by three other *khalīfas*, one of the latter being Abū Bakr al-Ghadāmsī, in later years a key figure in Dār Fūr-Sanūsiyya relations. In addition to their tasks as founders of a *zāwiya* and their diplomatic roles vis-à-vis `Alī Dīnār's government, the Sanūsī agents in al-Fāshir were active in trade.[57]

The initial period of positive relations between `Alī Dīnār and the Sanūsiyya between 1898 and 1902 was brought to an abrupt end by the course of events in Wadai. By the close of the nineteenth century the two large neighboring kingdoms of Dār Fūr and Wadai had experienced a long history of involvement in each other's affairs, the quality of which had ranged from a remote and passing episode of dynastic unity to occasional bitter warfare; in 1900 comparatively peaceful relations had prevailed for over a century, but each government took it as a natural prerogative of regional *Realpolitik* to attempt to influence the political life of the other. It was `Alī Dīnār's singular good fortune to come to the throne of Dār Fūr during the very year in which died Sultan Yūsuf Muḥammad Sharīf (1874-1898), the last strong and uncontested ruler of Wadai, whose passsing precipitated an extended period of civil strife. While the full story of the ensuing struggle for power in Wadai lies beyond the scope of this study, it is important in that it not only freed the new Dār Fūr monarch from the perennial threat of Wadaian subversion, but also afforded him opportunities for intervention in the western kingdom in support of congenial factions.

`Alī Dīnār was not able to prevent the temporary succession of Sultan Yūsuf's son Ibrāhīm in 1898, but in early 1900 rival factions supported by Dār Fūr drove the new king from his capital; they soon captured him, and in blinding him to prevent his restoration, caused his death. Thereafter the candidate supported by `Alī Dīnār, Aḥmad al-Ghazālī, the son of the late Sultan `Alī, was duly invested as the ruler of Wadai in February 1901. Four months later, in a letter to the Anglo-Egyptian authorities in Khartoum, `Alī Dīnār took personal credit for the success of Aḥmad al-Ghazālī:

[57] NRO Darfur 1/33/170 and NRO Intelligence 2/15/125.

> Delay in sending mail and news is due to the trouble recently in Dar Borgu [Wadai]. Great events have taken place there, which caused the death of many, and the end was the murder of their Sultan and the appointment of another in his place. They have written to me stating all that happened and I have sent them orders. At present there is trouble between the two parties over the choice of one who is fit to be Sultan. As they are obedient to my orders, and in order to end their troubles, I have selected Aḥmad al-Ghazālī, and have sent my orders with some of my men, who have left with the messengers sent by them. There is no doubt that on their arrival, the trouble will be over.[58]

Modest but significant testimony to the good relations that prevailed between Ali Dīnār and Aḥmad al-Ghazālī during 1901 may be seen in a pair of fortuitously surviving *laissez-passers* issued by the latter to parties of merchants bound for Dār Fūr via the road east through Dār Tāmā.[59] While the specific traders named have not been identified, they were probably members of the central Saharan merchant diaspora based in Wadai--the sort of men who at this period were indeed appearing in al-Fāshir, some of them loyal to the Sanūsiyya, and a few its official representatives.

If Sultan Muḥammad Sharīf's premonition that the establishment of a Sanūsī *zāwiya* in Wadai would lead to the overthrow of his kingdom by the foreign partisans it housed was perhaps exaggerated, it is certainly true that over the ensuing years of liberal rule in Wadai the leaders of the Sanūsiyya, no less than the rulers of neighboring Dār Fūr, had built up strong vested interests in Abesher. The Sanūsiyya, like `Alī Dīnār, played an active and controversial role in the events that followed the death of Sultan Yūsuf in 1898. Like `Alī Dīnār, the Sanūsī faction had little sympathy for Yūsuf's unfortunate and short-lived successor Sultan Ibrāhīm, and they acquiesced in his downfall. In contrast to `Alī Dīnār, however, their preferred candidate to replace Ibrāhīm was not Aḥmad al-Ghazālī, but another prince named Muḥammad Ṣāliḥ,* more

[58] Theobald, *'Alī Dīnār*, p. 60; NRO Intelligence 7/3/3.

[59] Kapteijns and Spaulding, *After the Millennium*, Docs. 26 and 27, pp. 154-160.

commonly known by his nickname, the "Lion of Murra."[60] Dūd Murra and the Sanūsiyya were unable to prevent the enthronement of Aḥmad al-Ghazālī, (who promptly retaliated against his Sanūsī opponents by closing the roads north),[61] but the Sanūsī faction never accepted his rule; even Aḥmad al-Ghazālī's patron `Alī Dīnār, as has been seen, was obliged to admit in his letter of June 1901 that the trouble in Wadai was not yet over, and that the civil war continued.

In November 1901, after only ten months of rule, Aḥmad al-Ghazālī was driven from the capital by Dūd Murra and the Sanūsī faction. He continued to resist, with `Alī Dīnār's backing, until June 1902, when his victorious opponents captured, blinded and executed him.[62] News of the death of `Alī Dīnār's protégé at the hands of the Sanūsī-backed faction in Wadai during June of 1902 must have reached al-Fāshir only days after notice of the passing of Sayyid al-Mahdī at Gouro on the second of that month. Liberated from the intimidating influence of that prestigious religious eminence, `Alī Dīnār felt free to retaliate against the organization that had so effectively thwarted his ambitions in Wadai. The incipient Sanūsī establishment in Dār Fūr was abruptly closed down and its agents deported. As Anglo-Egyptian records put it, "Before the middle of 1902, a rumor got about that the Senussi [al-Mahdī] had died, and Ali Dinar at once expelled all the Senussites from Fasher." The period of early accommodation between `Alī Dīnār and the Sanūsiyya was over. "Not unnaturally," the distant but attentive spymaster in Khartoum added, "we now find a gap in the course of the relations between [the] head of the Senussia and Ali Dinar lasting for some years."[63]

Among the several contenders for the throne of Wadai on the death of Sultan Yūsuf was Adam Asīl, a grandson of Sultan Muḥammad Sharīf. Although Asīl, like his rivals, had his followers among the Wadaian elite, he enjoyed the support of neither `Alī Dīnār nor the Sanūsiyya. When his refusal to accept the rule of another became apparent--it was said that he swore not to

[60] Document 8.

[61] Kapteijns and Spaulding, *After the Millennium*, p. 154; NRO Intelligence 2/15/125. The break was not detected by Triaud ("Relations," pp. 844-846, 871-896), who argues that the Sanūsiyya were neutral in the succession dispute. `Alī Dīnār did not agree.

[62] Theobald, *'Alī Dīnār*, p. 61.

[63] NRO Darfur 1/3/16.

cut his hair until achieving the throne--the stronger factions drove him from the capital. During 1900 Asīl fled west into Wadai's remote and recently annexed dependencies adjoining Lake Chad. There he encountered a complex and shifting vortex of diverse forces that offered a broad spectrum of opportunities and dangers to an exiled royal pretender in search of allies. Initially, few of Asīl's prospects seemed promising. The newly founded Sanūsī *zāwiya* at Bir Alali north of the lake was unlikely to offer sanctuary to an opponent of Dūd Murra. Scarcely more appealing was the major power in the region at the beginning of 1900, the warlord Rābiḥ Faḍl Allāh, who had marched west out of the Nile valley Sudan wrecking havoc across southern Wadai during the 1880s before moving on to seize Baghirmi and conquer Bornu. Another set of prospects lay with the advancing forces of imperial Europe, whose invisible web of paper claims was being cast across the central Sahara in distant capitals, to be realized piecemeal on African soil by marching columns of armed men in the years to come.

Asīl could not have known that by an agreement of 1893 most of Rābiḥ's Bornu had been appropriated sight-unseen by Britain, while the warlord's very capital in theory now belonged to a new German colony recently founded along the remote Atlantic coast of Kamerun by none other than his own uncle `Alī's erstwhile guest in Abesher, Gustav Nachtigal. Highly visible to Asīl and others, however, was the advance of the French, who had figured significantly in the political calculations of the region for some time.[64] By an agreement with Britain in 1899 France had laid claim on paper to what lay east of the Shari and west of the Nile watershed, including Wadai but not Dār Fūr, which latter was relinquished to Britain. It remained to assert a tangible French presence. During 1900 French forces dispatched months before from Brazzaville, Algiers and Dakar accomplished a coordinated assault upon Rābiḥ, and destroyed his state at Kousseri on 22 April. Later that year they established a *Territoire militaire des pays et protectorats du Tchad* through which to organize and administer anticipated conquests to follow. In the plans of the French there was indeed a place for Asīl; he was persuaded to submit, but soon had second thoughts, and was thereupon placed under arrest indefinitely until his new masters might stand in need of his services.

[64]Kapteijns and Spaulding, *After the Millennium*, Doc. 69, pp. 345-349.

Rābiḥ was not the only victim of the French military advances that culminated at Kousseri. The march across southern Algeria and Niger decisively tipped the scales in a longstanding struggle among Tuareg* factions in favor of those who sided with the Europeans, notably the Kel Owi of Aïr, at the expense of the Tuareg elite of Damergu.[65] The victims appealed to the Sanūsiyya for permission to seek refuge from the French in the shadow of Bir Alali, and this was granted; between April 1900 and June 1901 the leading shaykhs of the Ikaskazan and Imuzurag of Damergu led their people east into Kanem.[66] In the eastern lands the Tuareg immigrants were usually known by their Teda ethnonym, "Kinīn."*[67] The veiled newcomers, who numbered several thousands, proved an immediate and permanent source of profound aggravation to most of the older inhabitants of the Sanūsī world, who seem to have found their ways arrogant, bloodthirsty and thievish.[68] In the eyes of the Sanūsī masters, however, the Kinīn had earned a status of special religious merit by virtue of having made the *hijra* out of the land of thhe infidel into *Dār al-Islām*.[69] Moreover, they came to the Sanūsiyya as a disciplined and experienced warrior elite at the very moment when the creation of a Sanūsī military capability over and above the services of the order's brethren, or *ikhwān*,* seemed to have become a pressing necessity. For many years to come groups of refugee Tuareg under later leaders such as Ṣāliḥ Abū Karīm*[70] would continue to serve the Sanūsiyya as a corps of "troupes d'élite;" meanwhile, during 1901, the newcomers were sent out on reconnaissance patrols, instructed in the proper tactical use of firearms, and assigned to the reprovisioning of Bir Alali's stock of gunpowder.[71]

[65] See Baier, "Damergu."

[66] Triaud, *Tchad*, p. 52; see also Doc. 2, pp. 87-88.

[67] Kapteijns and Spaulding, *After the Millennium*, Docs. 31 and 32, pp. 178-185.

[68] Document 8; Triaud, *Tchad*, pp. 53-56.

[69] Document 18.

[70] Documents 11 and 18; Kapteijns and Spaulding, *After the Millennium*, Doc. 30, pp. 173-177 and Doc. 32, pp. 182-185; Triaud, "Relations," pp. 1056-1057; 1208-1220; 1739.

[71] Triaud, *Tchad*, pp. 53-56.

In the autumn of 1901 Sayyid al-Mahdī summoned to Gouro for consultation his master of the *zāwiya* of Bir Alali. Sīdī al-Barrānī, during his absence, entrusted the *zāwiya* to Ibrāhīm al-Gharbī, who may have hoped to become the permanent master through his superior's departure.[72] Thus it happened that Ibrāhīm al-Gharbī was in charge at Bir Alali on 9 November 1901 when a force sent out by the new French commander for Chad arrived there to add the Sanūsī outpost to the French empire. The intruders were ambushed outside the *zāwiya* and defeated.[73] Not long after, Sīdī al-Barrānī returned to Bir Alali from Gouro and Ibrāhīm al-Gharbī relinquished his command; a few weeks later the *zāwiya* fell to a stronger French force on 20 January 1902. Thus began the memorable struggle for Chad between the Europeans and the Sanūsiyya, which reached a turning point on 2 June 1909 with the fall of the capital of Wadai; Dūd Murra fled north to seek refuge with his Sanūsī friends, while Asīl, released from confinement for the occasion by the French, became a king of sorts at last.

Meanwhile, four months after the outbreak of hostilities between the Sanūsiyya and France at Bir Alali, Sayyid al-Mahdī died. The transition to a new generation of Sanūsī leadership was smoothed by the venerable guiding presence of Aḥmad al-Rīfī, who had played a similar role long before for al-Mahdī himself at the death of the Grand Sanūsī. Sayyid Aḥmad al-Sharīf, al-Mahdī's nephew, was chosen to lead the order during the difficult years to come. Before the end of 1902 he transferred the headquarters of the Sanūsiyya from Gouro back to Kufra, being motivated largely by the logistical difficulties of sustaining a major *zāwiya* amidst the very limited natural resources of Tibesti, and perhaps also by strategic and diplomatic considerations.[74]

The worldly affairs of the order were reorganized to accommodate the temporal aspirations of all seven principal heirs to the Grand Sanūsī's mantle. "It began to be the custom," as E.E. Evans-Pritchard put it,

> to earmark the surplus revenues of particular lodges [*zāwiyas*] for particular members of the Sanusi family, and these members became regarded as patrons of the lodges which supplied them and responsible

[72]Triaud, *Tchad*, p. 46; Doc. 21, pp. 134-136 and Doc. 27, pp. 146-147.

[73]Ibid., pp. 22-26.

[74]Evans-Pritchard, *The Sanusi*, p. 27; Triaud, *Tchad*, p. 68; "Relations," p. 1037ff.

> for their supervision. The territories in which the Order was dominant began to fall into spheres of influence controlled by individual members of the family, the allocation of spheres tending to be determined by the maternal kinship of the individual members.[75]

Relevant to the present study was Muḥammad `Ābid's special link to the *zāwiyas* of the Fazzān;[76] with that minor exception the correspondence between `Alī Dīnār and the Sanūsiyya betrays no inkling of doubt that between 1902 and 1916 the affairs of the order were directed by a single hand, and normally from Kufra.

An issue of comparatively minor significance to the new generation of Sanūsī leaders, but a matter of some importance for their historians, was the creation for them of new instruments with which to seal their official documents.[77] Aḥmad al-Sharīf and Muḥammad `Ābid had already possessed and used seals while at Gouro during the lifetime of al-Mahdī.[78] Upon his passing, however, both had new ones made--Muḥammad `Ābid in 1320/1902-1903[79] and Aḥmad al-Sharīf in 1321/1903-1904;[80] `Alī al-Khaṭṭābī

[75]Evans-Pritchard, *The Sanusi*, p. 77.

[76]Documents 22, 25 and 26.

[77]A reading and translation of the Grand Sanūsī's seal has been given by Klopfer (*Bewegung*, pp. 44, 70); Joseph Neigel's translation of the seal of al-Mahdī has been published by Triaud (*Tchad*, p. 82).

[78]Muḥammad `Ābid had a seal and used it on a letter of 25 Rabī` II 1318/23 July 1900 (Triaud, *Tchad*, Doc. 4, pp. 92-94 and Plate III). The seal text cannot be read from the plate, nor did Neigel propose a reading; however, it is not a seal that appears in the present collection. Aḥmad al-Sharīf had a seal and used it on a letter of Dhu'l-Qa`da 1318/February-March 1901 (Triaud, *Tchad*, Doc. 10, pp. 107-109 and Plate VII); indeed, the impressions of two different seals appear on this document. Neither seal text can be read from the plate, and no translation is given; however, it is not likely that either of them, being available in 1318, could be the one that appears in the present collection, which is clearly dated 1321/1903-1904.

[79]Documents 2, 3, 6 and 7; for the gift of a new seal from `Alī Dīnār, see Document 8.

[80]Documents 4, 10, 13, 14 and 20.

followed in 1322/1904-1905.[81] The seal used by Muḥammad Idrīs during this period also appears in the present collection, but the impression is very faint and the authors have not been able to read it.[82] These seal dates are the earliest fixed chronological points of reference to be found in the present collection of documents.

The years 1902-1909 were a period of gestation vital to the rebirth of cooperative relations between Dār Fūr and the Sanūsiyya, yet they are but poorly documented in regard to this theme. The information presently available may be arranged to clarify the overall historical context within which decisions were taken, but it does not suffice to elucidate the specific circumstances and motives that precipitated the resumption of ties between al-Fāshir and Kufra late in 1905.

In the west the French remained a major concern to the new Sanūsī leadership of 1902. During the first months after assuming the mantle of al-Mahdī, Aḥmad al-Sharīf seems to have directed a vain written appeal for support to the equivocating prince Asīl, whose armed entourage enjoyed strategic proximity to the French, and by year's end he had mustered the *ikhwān* and their allies for an attempt to retake Bir Alali by direct assault. When this attack failed on 4 December 1902, however, he shifted to a defensive posture; the Sanūsiyya now established fortified and well-provisioned bases at many of the oases of northern Chad, the foremost of these being placed at `Ayn Galakka ("Kalaka"*). A call went out to the Islamic faithful of the French-occupied southlands, summoning them to perform the *hijra* northward into Sanūsī-controlled territory. For the moment the French were unable to respond, but in mid-1904, with the formation of a corps of camel-mounted infantry, they initiated a bitter two-year struggle for the allegiance of the pastoral peoples of central Chad, many of whose patterns of seasonal transhumance obliged them to cross the invisible, newly-drawn frontier between the Sanūsiyya and the French. As months passed the French ventured deeper into the north; by the first of June 1906 they had overrun the Sanūsī post at the oasis of Voun

[81] Documents 5 and 17.

[82] Document 18.

(subsequently Faya Largeau) and were positioning themselves to assail `Ayn Galakka itself.[83] While direct evidence is lacking, it is clear that between 1902 and 1906 French pressure would have given the Sanūsiyya ample incentive to encourage warmer relations with Dār Fūr. The major impediment to this Sanūsī objective remained the cool relations prevailing between Dār Fūr and the brotherhood's longstanding southern ally, Wadai.[84]

Dūd Murra, the new ruler of Wadai, proved himself from the outset a reliable friend to Sanūsī interests, opening Wadai to the activities of foreign private traders and assuming responsibility for enforcing all credit obligations undertaken during the reign of his rival and predecessor Aḥmad al-Ghazālī.[85] Traders from Dār Fūr were by no means excluded; on the contrary, through a fortuitously-surviving *laissez-passer* of 1902 Dūd Murra extended his special protection to one of `Alī Dīnār's own royal commercial agents to ensure his safe return with goods from Wadai to Dār Fūr via Dār Tāma and Dār Qimr.[86] In contrast to Dūd Murra, however, `Alī Dīnār held to time-honored royal commercial prerogatives and did not open his kingdom to private enterprise, and his unwillingness to reciprocate the Wadaian policy of *laissez-faire* soon precipitated a new crisis over trade during 1904. From the perspective of a distant but attentive European observer, it seemed that `Alī Dīnār had refused "de concéder l'exemption des taxes aux caravanes venant du Ouaddaï alors que celui-ci la concède à Ali Dinar, sultan du Darfour."[87] Retrospective sources interior to the kingdom added the significant details that the Dār Fūr sultan had "illtreated the merchants from Wadai forcing them to sell their goods at prices

[83]Summarized from Ciammaichella, *Libyens et Français*, pp. 83ff.

[84]Ciammaichella (*Libyens et Français*, p. 89) concluded that during this period, "La politique suivie [by the Sanūsiyya] par rapport à Ali Dinar, sultan du Darfour, reste toujours celle d'une médiation entre Abéché et el-Facher."

[85]Max Adrian Simon von Oppenheim, in C.D. Joos, "Le Ouadai, Le Dar el Kouti et la Senoussia en 1904: Matèriaux pour étude de l'histoire des États d'Afrique Centrale," *Études Camerounaises*, No. 53-54 (octobre-décembre, 1956), 4-5.

[86]Kapteijns and Spaulding, *After the Millennium*, Doc. 28, pp. 161-163.

[87]Ciammaichella, *Libyens et Français*, p. 109, based on a report of 16 December 1904 by G. Mondello, Italian Vice-Consul at Benghazi, to his superior in Tripoli.

fixed by him, which were less than their cost price."[88] (Such perceptions of grievance on the part of private merchants were a common feature of the dynamic of political economy when commercial capitalism encountered the administered precapitalist economies of northeast African kingdoms.)[89] In response to `Alī Dīnār's handling of merchants from Wadai, Dūd Murra closed the road to Dār Fūr; he kept it closed for at least two years, and quite probably thereafter also until the fall of his kingdom in 1909.[90]

The strained trade relations that prevailed between Wadai and Dār Fūr after 1904 denied `Alī Dīnār access to Mediterranean markets via the Sanūsī-dominated central Saharan trading network, whose closest entrepot was Abesher, and left him dependent upon the caravans he himself might dispatch, at his own risk, northeastward to Upper Egypt down the old Forty Days' Road. Unfortunately, at precisely this moment the isolated oases north and east of Dār Fūr, together with the rich seasonal grazing lands that surrounded some of them, were targeted for conquest by the able and acquisitive young Shaykh `Alī al-Tōm of the Kabābīsh. Shaykh `Alī not only directed the might of the dominant pastoral community beyond northern Dār Fūr's eastern frontier, but also enjoyed the uncritical and unquestioning support of the Anglo-Egyptian authorities in Khartoum. During 1905 the Kabābīsh cut the Forty Days' Road at the oasis of Bīr Naṭrūn and thereafter, as it became increasingly clear that `Alī Dīnār's repeated protests to Khartoum would be systematically ignored, their predatory incursions increased in scale and intensity.[91] The Forty Days' Road was not secure to caravans from Dār Fūr.

[88]Lidwien Kapteijns, *Mahdist Faith and Sudanic Tradition: The History of the Masālīt Sultanate, 1870-1930* (London: Routledge and Kegan Paul, 1985), p. 174.

[89]For a discussion see Kapteijns, "The Organization of Exchange," and Kapteijns and Spaulding, "Pre-Colonial Trade."

[90]Kapteijns, *Mahdist Faith*, p. 174.

[91]For the initial attacks on Bīr Naṭrūn during 1905 see Theobald, *`Alī Dīnār*, pp. 73-75; a more detailed treatment of the conflict as it developed in the years to follow may be found in Talal Asad, *The Kababish Arabs: Power, Authority and Consent in a Nomadic Tribe* (New York: Praeger, 1970), pp. 161-167.

During the later months of 1905, with access to Mediterranean markets severed or endangered along both eastern and western routes, `Alī Dīnār turned directly to the Sanūsiyya--"opening a correspondence with the Arabs of Kufra," as Anglo-Egyptian intelligence put it--in "an attempt to give a fillip to the trade in arms, a commodity which [he] was finding it harder and harder to obtain."[92] The Sanūsi authorities responded promptly; the first caravan from Kufra reached al-Fāshir early in 1906, arms were delivered to `Alī Dīnār, and an era of renewed interaction between Dār Fūr and the Sanūsiyya began.[93] It is highly probable that from the beginning these exchanges were accompanied by a correspondence, now lost, similar to the letters of the present collection; for example, Anglo-Egyptian intelligence mentioned the existence of a letter of 13 Dhu'l-Qa`da 1325/18 December 1907 in which Aḥmad al-Rīfī acknowledged the receipt of letters and a consignment of goods from `Alī Dīnār.[94] Similarly the present collection, while it contains all the letters available to the authors, is clearly not a complete record of Dār Fūr-Sanūsiyya correspondence.

`Alī Dīnār's new road to the Sanūsiyya led 950 miles due north from al-Fāshir to Kufra across very rugged desert terrain. Since delay was rarely advantageous and frequently fatal to travelers it was normal to press forward with all deliberate speed, the latter a matter concerning which the camels upon which the traffic depended had their own preconceived and time-honored opinions; a normal journey between Kufra and al-Fāshir took about two months.[95] Several alternative routes were available. While direct evidence is

[92]NRO Darfur 1/3/16.

[93]An Anglo-Egyptian spy in al-Fāshir claimed that `Alī Dīnār received 1,670 rifles and 83,500 rounds of ammunition from the Sanūsī between May 1906 and April 1910 (Theobald, *`Alī Dīnār*, p. 59); these figures were greatly exaggerated.

[94]NRO Intelligence 5/3/40; the officer translating the brief precis of this letter after the fall of Dār Fūr noted that it was ten years old.

[95]A.M. Hassanein covered this distance going south between 18 April and 19 June 1923 (*The Lost Oases*, [New York: Century, 1925], p. 178); the Sanūsī agent Faraj Khalīfa left al-Fāshir on or about 18 October 1911 and arrived in Kufra near the end of Dhu'l-Ḥijja on 21 December (Doc. 16).

lacking, it seems likely that before 1914, while the Sanūsiyya controlled northeastern Chad, many caravans would have swung west to take advantage of the deep well at Sarra, dug at the command of al-Mahdī to facilitate passage of the most difficult stage of the desert crossing.[96] On the other hand, it is certain that the final caravan recorded below, late in 1915, struck east and then south to intersect the Forty Days' Road at the oasis of Nukhayla ("Merga"*) before turning southwestward to al-Fāshir.[97] The path followed by A.M. Hassanein Bey in 1923 exemplified a viable middle course between these eastern and western extremes.[98] When a northward-bound caravan from al-Fāshir reached Kufra, the Mediterranean coast still lay an additional 700 miles farther, across similarly harsh desert. It was therefore judicious for travelers from either north or south to exchange their tired camels in Kufra before proceeding. Unfortunately the immediate environs of Kufra did not support large numbers of camels, so that although the oasis settlement was a major center for the transshipment of goods and the resupply of transport, it was almost totally dependent in regard to the latter upon camels imported either from the distant Cyrenaican uplands or the even more remote Sudan.[99]

The pattern of direct commercial exchange between `Alī Dīnār and the Sanūsiyya instituted in 1905 became firmly established over the next several years, and by the close of 1908 the two governments were ready for closer and more formal relations. An important incentive to rapprochement at this time was provided by the French, who throughout 1907 and 1908 began to launch attacks against `Ayn Galakka and other Sanūsī posts in northern Chad and unleashed Asīl, their captive would-be sultan of Wadai, to assail Dūd Murra from the west. `Alī Dīnār responded by inviting Kufra to smooth out the differences between Dār Fūr and its powerful western neighbor; "it was reported in Khartoum that he had sent twenty delegates to the Sanūsī leader to ask him to mediate between the

[96]This exploit soon became the stuff of pious legend; see Forbes, *Kufara*, p. 228; Triaud, "Relations," pp. 820-821.

[97]Document 24; Triaud, "Relations," p. 812, note 20.

[98]Hassanein, *The Lost Oases*; see map facing p. 8.

[99]Ibid., p. 103.

two sultans, and to exchange ivory for firearms and ammunition."[100] The correspondence preserved here began.

At first encounter, the uninitiated reader will probably be impressed with the passion and ingenuity invested by the Sanūsī correspondents in the creation of the elaborate titles, epithets and expressions of admiration through which they addressed `Alī Dinār. A useful perspective on this unfamiliar mode of expression was proposed by Rosita Forbes, who visited Kufra at the close of 1920. "I think utter simplicity and little speech are the best methods of approach [to the Sanūsī]," she concluded. "Flowery words impress them, and they say, 'Thy conversation is like honey. Allow me to return that I may drink of it.' But to themselves they murmur, 'He is a juggler of words. Let us be careful lest he bemuse us!'"[101] In at least one instance the efflorescence of Sanūsī rhetoric concealed an expression of deeper resonance; the occasionally-recurring phrase, "at every glance and breath, as many as God's wisdom accommodates," was borrowed from the "great *wird*" or devotional litany of the Sanūsiyya, deriving ultimately from the customary idiom of the Grand Sanūsī's teacher, Aḥmad b. Idrīs al-Fāsī.[102]

Documents 2 through 7, written in Kufra during the last quarter of 1908, contained Sanūsī responses to `Alī Dīnār's new diplomatic initiative--though they also addressed a variety of other concerns both personal and commercial. Documents 2 and 3 were intended to accompany a southbound caravan of November-December 1908 led by `Abd al-Qādir al-Azraq,* while Documents 4 through 7 were written at the close of the year for a second caravan under Muḥammad Yūnus* that probably left Kufra in January 1909. Both sets of letters mentioned the anticipated arrival from the south of a caravan led by Faraj [Khalīfa]* and Ghayth [Abū Karīm],* which however did not reach Kufra before the end of the year.

[100]Kapteijns, *Mahdist Faith*, p. 174.

[101]Forbes, *Kufara*, p. 107.

[102]R.S. O'Fahey, *Enigmatic Saint: Ahmad Ibn Idris and the Idrisi Tradition* (London: Hurst, 1990), facing p. 1; Triaud, *Tchad*, p. 174.

On the diplomatic front, `Alī Dīnār had asked for the return to Dār Fūr of Abū Bakr al-Ghadāmsī, the veteran diplomat who had represented Sanūsī interests in al-Fāshir during the earlier period of close relations. The Sanūsī leaders were eager to comply, "so that through his presence, God willing, there would be guidance and support for those parts" (Doc. 4); "Our order is that he should stay in the vicinity of your places to be an intermediary between us and you" (Doc. 2). The emissary was promptly summoned from elsewhere in the Sanūsī world, but had not come to Kufra in time to accompany the caravan of `Abd al-Qādir al-Azraq; however, with hasty preparation he succeeded in joining the party of Muḥammad Yūnus (Doc. 7). Meanwhile the Sanūsī leaders were punctilious in regard to an often-sensitive point of diplomatic protocol, the delay of foreign messengers; a special letter (Doc. 3) was prepared to excuse `Alī Dīnār's courier for having remained in Kufra to celebrate the *`Īd al-Fiṭr*.[103] Finally, (a frustration to historians), the authorities in Kufra entrusted some of their more important messages to be conveyed orally by their agents in person (Docs. 4, 6).[104]

The exchange of greetings and presents among rulers constituted a sphere of discourse in which diplomacy merged with personal affairs and commerce.[105] Letters of `Alī al-Khaṭṭābī (Doc. 5) and Muḥammad `Ābid (Doc. 6) were largely barren of overtly material concerns and served primarily to maintain friendly contacts; elsewhere, however, Muḥammad `Ābid thanked `Alī Dīnār for presents sent to the Sanūsī children (Doc. 2), noted the dispatch of a horse as a return gift (Doc. 7), and specifically requested butter for medicinal purposes and the complete skins of tropical cats (Doc. 2). Of more fundamental importance, of course, were the major caravan shipments of Sudanese goods and the arms and ammunition offered in return, and these received courteous attention, directly or obliquely, throughout the correspondence. The Sanūsī leadership

[103]Kapteijns and Spaulding, *After the Millennium*, p. 30.

[104]See also Triaud, *Tchad*, p. 83.

[105]Kapteijns and Spaulding, *After the Millennium*, pp. 22-31.

also raised the delicate question of how the private traders sent to Dār Fūr under their patronage, "those of the Majābra . . . who seek magnanimous compassion" (Doc. 4), would be treated in an economically conservative African kingdom. That all was not entirely well may be inferred from the reference (Doc. 7) to "people awaiting slaves" whose needs required "urgent attention very, very quickly." But Kufra had faith in `Alī Dīnār's version of *glasnost*: "If God wills, we will encourage the merchants and write to them to bring weapons to your beautiful land" (Doc. 2). Meanwhile, the delay of Muḥammad Yūnus in Kufra to strengthen his camels (Doc. 6) testified both to the rigors of the desert crossing and the frequent difficulty or impossibility of obtaining fresh transport at the oasis.

When Abū Bakr al-Ghadāmsī reached al-Fāshir, probably with the caravan of Muḥammad Yūnus in about March 1909, he established a permanent Sanūsī presence there. `Alī Dīnār treated the Sanūsī ambassador well. "The ease and goodness that I saw from our lord the sultan I never saw before even from my father," the diplomat reported to Kufra, "for truly I am in splendid repose with him. May God be aware of this and recompense him with the best of rewards" (Doc. 13). Although this embassy or *zāwiya* did not figure prominently in subsequent correspondence between `Alī Dīnār and Kufra, it did attract the scrutiny of Anglo-Egyptian intelligence, particularly in later years as the passions leading to World War I reached their climax. In 1915 spies said that "Abu Bakr el Ghadamsi . . . is allowed to live quietly in El Fasher, and minister to such [Sanūsī devotees] as need his offices, but probably owes his immunity from interference to the fact that he lives a fairly secluded and unostentatious existence."[106] It was correctly reported that he had been in al-Fāshir for about seven years, acting as a commercial agent for the Sanūsiyya, and that he lived in a big house with his large family. Considerably less plausible, though richly indicative of the temper of the times, was the fear expressed in Khartoum that he might be a Bolshevik--the bearer of a "red complex"--because of the color of his *ṭarbūsh* (cap).[107]

[106]NRO Darfur 1/3/16.

[107]Ibid.

Document 8 is Muḥammad `Ābid's addendum or postscript to another letter to `Alī Dīnār that is now lost; it is not dated, but may be placed in the last half of 1909 or the first quarter of 1910 on the basis of internal evidence. In an unusually frank intrusion into the internal affairs of Dār Fūr, the Sanūsī leader extended specific approval to the sultan's policies in regard to two important and potentially controversial issues of that year, the fall of Sinīn Ḥusayn* and of Dūd Murra.

Sinīn Ḥusayn was an Islamic holy man of Tāma ethnic origin who joined the army of the Mahdist state of the Sudan and rose through the ranks during service in the Nuba mountains and Ethiopia. In November 1896 he was left in command of a residual Mahdist garrison at Kabkābiyya in northern Dār Fūr when the provincial governor withdrew the bulk of the western army to face the Anglo-Egyptian invasion at Omdurman.[108] Sinīn did not recognize the restored Dār Fūr sultanate of `Alī Dīnār, and for a decade he repulsed repeated attacks by the king's forces. But in 1907 the sultan sent his main army and leading generals to surround Kabkābiyya, and the holdout Mahdist enclave fell after a bitter seventeen-month siege early in January 1909.[109] The Sanūsiyya had never sought close relations with the Mahdist state,[110] but it is nevertheless noteworthy that the authorities in Kufra chose to regard Sinīn and his followers as rebels against `Alī Dīnār rather than zealous Muslims worthy of compassion.

Abesher fell to the French-backed forces of Asīl on 2 June 1909, and Dūd Murra withdrew northward from his capital to Kapka; there, over the next ten months, he mustered a force of Wadaian loyalists and Sanūsī partisans with which to counterattack. In this resistance he enjoyed the wholehearted support of Kufra and the somewhat more equivocal endorsement of `Alī Dīnār; by April 1910 the two sultans had assembled formidable armies to oppose the French and attempted to coordinate their operations, but were defeated in separate engagements on the seventh (Dār Fūr) and the nineteenth (Dūd Murra).[111]

108 Kapteijns, *Mahdist Faith*, p. 103.

109 Samuel Bey Atiyah, "Senin and Ali Dinar," *Sudan Notes and Records* VII, 2 (1924), 63-69.

110 P.M. Holt, *The Mahdist State in the Sudan*, 2nd ed. (Oxford: Clarendon, 1970), pp. 112-113; Ziadeh, *Sanūsīya*, pp. 51-58.

111 Kapteijns and Spaulding, *After the Millennium*, Docs. 29-33, pp. 164-191.

During the critical weeks leading up to these battles, the Sanūsiyya was represented at the court of `Alī Dīnār by a special envoy, the eminent diplomat Ibrāhīm al-Gharbī (Docs. 10, 12). Following his defeat before Kapka, Dūd Murra retreated southward into Dār Masālīt; a wave of western refugees fled into Dār Fūr, and a new episode in the international relations of the region began. During his months at Kapka Dūd Murra had received letters of support and offers of asylum from `Alī Dīnār; it seems likely that these are the messages for which Muḥammad `Ābid expressed gratitude.[112]

Conditions of abnormal drought and sustained hardship descended upon Cyrenaica and the Sudan in 1908 and increased thereafter, culminating in the great famine of 1913.[113] In Document 8 Muḥammad `Ābid specifically lamented these difficult circumstances: "during this year we have suffered much hardship due to the shortage of provisions for people. Even at the [Cyrenaican] coast people have complained much about this. May God give us a new year that is better!" Even at the best of times Kufra, like Gouro, relied to some extent upon its imports, and in a year when Wadai was lost to the French and Cyrenaica afflicted by famine, the Sanūsī leaders found themselves significantly

[112]For example, in a subsequent letter of 15 Shawwāl 1329/26 October 1911 Dūd Murra himself referred to friendly letters from `Alī Dīnār received before his retreat from Kapka; see NRO Intelligence 2/3/12.

[113]Drought and famine are matters of contemporary concern in the Sudan, and several scholars have explored historical dimensions to the problem. For the prolonged famine of the 1830s, see G.M. LaRue, "Terrible Droughts Followed by Famines:' Towards an Appreciation of the Role of Drought in the History of Dār Fūr, ca. 1750-1916," (unpublished paper). For the famine of "The Year Six," see Richard Pankhurst and Douglas H. Johnson, "The great drought and famine of 1888-92 in northeast Africa," in Douglas H. Johnson and David M. Anderson, eds., *The Ecology of Survival: Case Studies from Northeast African History* (Boulder: Westview, 1988), pp. 47-70. For the famine of 1913, see Kapteijns, *Mahdist Faith*, pp. 192-193, 203; for the earlier onset of this period of hardship in Cyrenaica, see W.H. Beehler, *The History of the Italian-Turkish War* (Annapolis: U.S. Naval Institute, 1913), p. 14. An extended but idiosyncratic and ahistorical treatment of recent Sudanese famine may be found in Alexander de Waal, *Famine that Kills: Darfur, Sudan, 1984-1985* (Oxford: Clarendon, 1989).

dependent upon the resources of `Alī Dīnār. "Had it not been for what has come to me through your generosity and great kindness," Muḥammad `Ābid wrote, "I do not know what would have happened to me." He expressed gratitude for what had already been delivered by Faraj Khalīfa, anticipation for what was on the way with Ghayth Abū Karīm, and encouragement for the prompt dispatch of a third caravan led by `Abd al-Qādir al-Azraq; he also introduced a new caravan leader, Aḥmad Bū Kāda al-Majābrī,* apparently not previously known to the sultan. Indicative of the hard times was the fact that Faraj, unable to obtain fresh transport in Kufra, had been obliged to break his journey at the oasis for a month before departing to the north--and even then at some risk to his tired camels. On a personal note, Muḥammad `Ābid offered discreet advice on the suitability of weapons as presents for the Sanūsī children, and thanked the king for the gift of a gun and a new seal. The latter, first used on this letter itself, made a large octagonal impression (Docs. 8, 12, 15, 16); it replaced a small, round seal with the same text (Docs. 2, 3, 6, 7).

Documents 9 (1 November 1909) and 10 (15 August 1910) expose aspects of `Alī Dīnār's northward trade. Dār Fūr's most significant export goods were slaves--destined largely for the Sanūsī settlements themselves--but above all, ivory for sale at the Mediterranean coast. Arms and ammunition were the essential imports, supplemented by a wide variety of luxury goods. The foreign trade of Dār Fūr is best understood as a royal monopoly; though there may well have been unseen violations on the part of private traders, the Sanūsī documents do not suggest that there was any merchant in Dār Fūr other than the king himself. The northerners who came to al-Fāshir to do business under Sanūsī patronage enjoyed no comparable corporate identity; each individual or team of kinsmen who dealt with the king performed their own calculations of loss or gain on the basis of exchange values at the respective termini of the long desert crossing.[114] In some cases the private traders from the north, including the Sanūsī leaders themselves, supplied venture capital and brought or sent goods south to be sold at their own risk; sometimes they brought currency with which

[114]For example, see the calculations offered by the Tripolitanian merchant Yūnus b. Abd al-Sayyid after his capture at Bir Alali; see Triaud, *Tchad*, p. 67.

to make purchases (Doc. 10).[115] In many instances, however, it was `Alī Dīnār who advanced goods on credit to the northerners, and anxiously awaited the outcome of their commercial endeavors at the distant coast. The task of the Sanūsī leadership in Kufra, insofar as the flow of commerce was concerned, was to authenticate the trustworthiness and probity of the men they sent south to Dār Fūr or north to the coast, and periodically to communicate the status of transactions involving the king's goods--transactions that were often large in magnitude and which inevitably took months to complete.

Document 9, a letter from the distinguished Sanūsī elder statesman Aḥmad al-Rīfī, provided a status report on one of `Alī Dīnār's royal ventures, assuring the king that his ivory had been received in Kufra, transshipped (with some difficulties in regard to transport), and exchanged in the north for munitions. Expressed obliquely was the assumption that since the Sanūsī had helped subsidize the transport of the king's goods, they had a right to a share of the profits. Document 10, from Aḥmad al-Sharīf, reported on the status of a similar transaction a year later. He also solicited the services of a scribe skilled in the handwriting of the eastern Arab world; it is significant and noteworthy that he anticipated the presence of such an individual in Dār Fūr.

The Sanūsī presence in the southlands was organized into a number of individual commands, each separately responsible to the center; most were based upon fertile oases whose lands and date palms, in significant part, belonged to the order as pious endowment. Following the fall of Bir Alali and the death of al-Mahdī in 1902, however, the new head of the brotherhood Aḥmad al-Sharīf gathered his ethnically heterogeneous pastoral followers, ostensibly to tend that portion of the order's endowed property comprised of livestock; he assigned them to the Ennedi region under the leadership of Ṣāliḥ Abū Karīm. This pastoral command of the Sanūsiyya in the southlands was called "the camp," or al-Dōr.[116] As the new French camel corps began its thrust northward from Lake Chad up the chain of Sanūsī oasis settlements, culminating in the fall of Voun in June 1906, Aḥmad al-Sharīf mobilized the

[115]The importation of currency into the kingdoms of the Sudan was a longstanding branch of commerce; see Spaulding, *Heroic Age*, pp. 142-145.

[116]Triaud, "Relations," pp. 1056-1057.

nomadic warriors of al-Dōr to undertake armed reprisals, which began late that year: "la montée en puissance des nomades des Dôr date de ce moment."[117] The formation of a well-armed and militant but imperfectly disciplined force on Dār Fūr's northwestern frontier would not have been viewed with equanimity by `Alī Dīnār, particularly as the elimination of Sinīn Ḥusayn and the fall of Kabkābiyya early in 1909 allowed the sultan to consolidate his grip on Dār Fūr's northwestern districts. Nor did the raiders of al-Dôr halt the advance of the French.

The months following the fall of Abesher brought turmoil to Dār Fūr's western frontier, for it was not self-evident that the French conquest of the Wadaian capital extended also to the sultanate's peripheral tributary states such as Dār Tāma, or indeed that the French would refrain from pushing on east into Dār Masālīt, a precariously-independent little buffer state that `Alī Dīnār regarded as his westernmost province. In the event, the reigning sultan of Dār Tāma was replaced by a client of Asīl; then, during February 1910 the ruler of Dār Masālīt, to divert the attention of the French, invaded Dār Tāma and overthrew its new government; a week later the French overran Dār Tāma and restored the previous ruler, only to be followed a few days later by `Alī Dīnār's generals, who restored the original Tāma sultan.[118] The situation was complicated by the proximity to the Tāma capital of Kapka, where Dūd Murra with the backing of the Sanūsiyya was mustering his Wadaian loyalists for a counterattack on Asīl and the French. Prominent among his generals at Kapka was the Tuareg leader Ṣāliḥ Abū Karīm, the Sanūsī governor of the Ennedi based on Beskere and the commander in battle of the Sanūsī *ikhwān* in the service of Dūd Murra.[119] Even as the Sanūsī diplomat Ibrāhīm al-Gharbī was in al-Fāshir attempting to help `Alī Dīnār and Dūd Murra to forge a united front against the French, however, correspondence from the field revealed considerable reluctance on the part of Dūd Murra's generals to make common cause with Dār Fūr--sentiments which `Alī Dīnār's intrusion into Tāma affairs would certainly have exacerbated. The westerners retaliated by raiding Dār Fūr for livestock and slaves and then fleeing back into

[117]Triaud, "Relations," p. 1089.

[118]Kapteijns, *Mahdist Faith*, pp. 183-186.

[119]Kapteijns and Spaulding, *After the Millennium*, p. 173.

Chad; Ṣāliḥ Abū Karīm, said the French, was transforming Beskere into an "Ali Baba's cave," filled with thieves.[120]

Document 11 is dated only to the year 1328/13 January 1919-1 January 1911, but it is probable that it was written in the context of Dār Fūr's intervention in Chadian affairs in March 1910, and specifically as a response to clashes with Ṣāliḥ Abū Karīm. `Alī Dīnār ordered the Tuareg leader to leave his realm forthwith--the sultan's characteristically blunt and vigorous idiom of expression contrasting sharply with the polite circumlocutions of Sanūsī rhetoric. Contrary to superficial appearances, however, this letter marked the beginning rather than the end of a relationship between the two leaders. In April 1910 Ṣāliḥ Abū Karīm fought beside Dūd Murra, and following the sultan's defeat he escorted him into exile in Dār Masālīt.[121] Then he returned to Beskere, and despite the harsh words recorded here, he cooperated fully with `Alī Dīnār throughout the rest of 1910 and early 1911 in enforcing a boycott on trade between Dār Fūr and French-occupied Wadai.

Meanwhile the authorities in Kufra attempted to reassert control over the Sanūsī pastoral command of al-Dōr. In letters now known only through very abbreviated English précis, Aḥmad al-Sharīf himself indicated his intention of making the long journey south from Kufra to visit al-Dōr late in 1909, and while it is doubtful that the master of the Sanūsiyya in fact came to al-Dōr in person, several of the younger Sayyids did; early in 1910 Idrīs, al-Riḍā and Ṣafī al-Dīn all wrote to `Alī Dīnār from al-Dōr.[122] Significantly, the letter of Idrīs sought to resolve a clash between private commercial enterprise and royally-regulated commerce; it "requested Ali Dinar to allow a man of theirs to sell the camels he [`Alī Dīnār] had prohibited to be sold for [the private Sanūsī merchant] not having had a note of introduction from them [the young Sayyids] previously."[123]

[120]Ciammaichella, *Libyens et Français*, p. 112; see also Kapteijns and Spaulding, *After the Millennium*, Doc. 31, pp. 178-181. An extended discussion of Tuareg raids out of the Ennedi and `Alī Dīnār's attempts to counter them may be found in NRO Intelligence 1/1/4 and NRO Intelligence 2/5/19.

[121]Kapteijns and Spaulding, *After the Millennium*, p. 182.

[122]NRO Intelligence 5/3/40.

[123]Ibid.

Following the defeat of Dūd Murra on 19 April 1910 a wave of western refugees poured into Dār Fūr. Some formally and definitively submitted to `Alī Dīnār; for example, the Wadaian *`aqīd al-Zabāda* Aḥmad* came to al-Fāshir, joined the sultan's court, and later played a conspicuous role in Dār Fūr - Sanūsiyya diplomacy (Docs. 28, 29).[124] Many of the newcomers, however, were not inclined to obey `Alī Dīnār, and were slow to abandon the vocation of holy warrior; conspicuous among these irreconcilables were the arch-militants of the Sanūsiyya, the Tuareg, who even before the fall of Abesher had taken to crossing northern Dār Fūr to raid the Kabbābish far to the east, and even the Ḥawāwīr whose homeland adjoined the Nile.[125] The turbulent westerners, however outspoken their Sanūsī loyalties, became a source of considerable irritation to `Alī Dīnār during 1910, and not even the authorities in Kufra were willing to defend their followers in the south. "They have grown tired and their spirits have failed in the absence of what promotes order," wrote Muḥammad `Ābid (Doc. 12), and he promised to notify the community of al-Dōr that they would henceforth be under `Alī Dīnār's oversight. (He also apologized for having been absent from Kufra for an extended period during 1910). By March 1911 the sultan had successfully asserted his control over al-Dōr, and earned the praises of Kufra for his responsible governance, notably the "opening of a road" southward west of Jabal Marra by which the Sanūsī partisans were allowed to tap the rich agricultural resources of Dār Masālīt (Doc. 13).[126] When the French invaded the Ennedi and seized Beskere in May 1911, Ṣāliḥ Abū Karīm sought refuge at the court of `Alī Dīnār.[127]

[124]At the fall of Abesher the *`aqīd* followed Dūd Murra to Kapka. He is mentioned by title, though not by name, as one of the authors of a letter of 5 March 1910 appealing to the powerful but then-vacillating *`aqīd al-Maḥāmīd* to join Dūd Murra in opposing Asīl and the French; see Kapteijns and Spaulding, *After the Millennium*, Doc. 29, pp. 164-172.

[125]NRO Intelligence 2/3/14.

[126]For the role of Dār Masālīt as a regional granary see Kapteijns, *Mahdist Faith*, pp. 25, 31-32.

[127]Kapteijns, *Mahdist Faith*, p. 195.

The "enemies of God" were on the march. `Alī Dīnār's steadfast (though not disinterested) support for Dūd Murra and his moderation in dealing with the Wadaian refugees during 1910 made a highly favorable impression in Kufra. "These days there is no place except yours there [south of the desert] upon which one can depend for the support of Islam," wrote Aḥmad al-Sharīf (Doc. 13), and he promised to redouble efforts to supply Dār Fūr with munitions. The Sānūsī leader also sent presents, notably books, and reported on the state of the king's commercial consignments.

Following the fall of Wadai French patrols pressed on into Dār Masālīt and other territories that `Alī Dīnār regarded as his own.[128] For three years and more the sultan appealed repeatedly to his nominal British overlords; after a decade of having faithfully delivered tribute to Khartoum, he now demanded the minimum of protection that his otherwise-distasteful dependent status must surely bear. In return, however, the king received nothing more than blandly condescending and temporizing letters; "`Alī Dīnār must have felt that he had been deserted and betrayed by the Sudan Government," concluded A.B. Theobald.[129] "If you are concerned for the welfare of this country," said the king in one of his last appeals, "you will at once take steps with the French Government to give us peace. Otherwise please leave us to die fighting them. It will be better to die for our faith and religion."[130]

Late in 1911 the king, abandoned by his nominal European overlords, took steps to strengthen his own ability to resist. He sent north to Kufra an unusually large shipment of ivory with instructions that the Sanūsī were "to obtain Remington ammunition, to supplement it for you with the [ammunition] of the Greeks, and that it should come quickly" (Doc. 150); the consignment

[128]Kapteijns, *Mahdist Faith*, pp. 180-197.

[129]Theobald, *`Alī Dīnār*, p. 103.

[130]Ibid., p. 102. It is possible, though unproven, that `Alī Dīnār mentioned his increasing disenchantment with "the people of the [Anglo-Egyptian] government" to the Sanūsī during 1911, and that oblique reference to this change in attitude may be found in Document 16.

was said to be worth 10,000 rounds.[131] It was delivered safely to Kufra on 21 December 1911 (Doc. 16) by a caravan led by Faraj Khalīfa (Doc. 15), followed shortly by a second courier with additional instructions (Doc. 16). Unfortunately the sultan's initiative found Kufra in a state of crisis. Documents 14, 15, 16 and 17 were written at the middle of January 1912 for dispatch south not long thereafter via a caravan to be led by Ghayth Bū Qandīl (Docs. 14, 15); they undertook to explain the delicate situation carefully to the distant king.

On 29 September 1911 Italy declared war on the Ottoman Empire, one objective being the seizure of Libya as a colony; Italian troops went ashore at Tripoli, Benghazi, Derna and Tobruk during October and established beachheads. News of the invasion reached Kufra in December (Doc. 15), and Aḥmad al-Sharīf, in his correspondence with ʿAlī Dīnār, wrote angrily of "God's enemy the Italians . . . vile unbelievers," and expressed the hope "May He [God] with your sword cut the throats of the faction of the depraved, deceitful unbelievers!" (Doc. 14). Yet at this initial stage the posture of the Sanūsiyya in regard to the new European invaders was more complex than long-term hindsight might suggest, for over the years the brotherhood had also experienced some difficulties with the previous masters of the coasts, the Ottomans--a relationship further troubled by the rise of the Young Turks in 1908, which brought to Libya such innovations as parliamentary elections and even the imposition of a Turkish administrator upon the Sanūsī spiritual citadel of Jaghbūb.[132] Some Italian partisans ventured to speculate that the Sanūsiyya might quietly welcome a Turkish defeat.[133] While Aḥmad al-Sharīf soon

[131]NRO Darfur 1/3/6. "He [ʿAlī Dīnār] traded with the Senussists on a deposit account," the intelligence officer explained. The report said that the consignment had been delivered by Muḥammad Yūnus, another experienced caravan leader on the Kufra-al-Fāshir road, but it is reasonably certain that the shipment delivered by Faraj Khalīfa is intended.

[132]See Michel LeGall, "The Ottoman Government and the Sanusiyya: A Reappraisal," *International Journal of Middle East Studies* XXI, 1 (1989), 91-106. LeGall concludes (p. 101) that 'relations between the [Sanūsī] *tariqa* and the Ottoman government were far more complicated and troubled than the current literature allows;" Triaud, "Relations," p. 814.

[133]For crude propaganda puffery to this effect, see Charles Lapworth, *Tripoli and Young Italy* (London: Swift, 1912), pp. 184-188 and Paulo De Vecchi, *Italy's Civilizing Mission in Africa* (New York: Brentano, 1912), p. 38.

proved these hopes utterly vain in regard to his Libyan homeland, he fully justified them in a quite different theater of the Italo-Turkish war--and did so by drawing upon the commercial resources of `Alī Dīnār's kingdom.

Long before, the Grand Sanūsī's spiritual master Aḥmad b. Idrīs al-Fāsī, during the latter years of his life (c. 1830-1837), had settled at Ṣabyā, then considered part of the Yemen though subsequently incorporated into `Asīr province of the kingdom of Saudi Arabia. In 1906 his great-grandson Muḥammad (d. 1923) launched a revolt against Ottoman rule in the Yemen. "The Idrīsī," as he was commonly known, had previously established contact with the Italian embassy in Cairo, and when Italy declared war on the Ottomans in 1911, she began to offer Muḥammad material aid.[134] The Idrīsī enjoyed considerable success in the field; "these insurgents put the Turkish forces of Yemen on the defensive and greatly relieved the Italians," one neutral military observer concluded.[135] They also placed Aḥmad al-Sharīf in the cleft of a moral dilemma: should he help the Turks defend Libya against Italy, or should he assist the Italians against them, in support of the Idrīsī, his spiritual kinsman by Sufi pedigree?

In the event, Aḥmad al-Sharīf found justification and means for waging the Italo-Turkish war from both sides, backing the Turks in Libya and the Italians in the Yemen. Given the circumstances, however, his tangible support for the Idrīsī was inevitably very limited. Sanūsī agents imported slaves from the Sudan to Kufra, whence they were sent out via the network of *zāwiyas* in the east to smuggle their human cargo disguised as wives and pilgrims to Mecca; there they were sold, the profits to be converted into munitions and delivered to the Idrīsī.[136] Given the brevity of the war and logistical constraints, it is clear that only a few such missions were in fact carried out, but they do suffice to demonstrate Aḥmad al-Sharīf's equivocal attitude toward Turkish rule and his determination to follow an independent course. Meanwhile, Aḥmad al-Sharīf summoned back to Kufra all the *ikhwān* who happened to be in Dār Fūr at the

[134]O'Fahey, *Enigmatic Saint*, pp. 119-125; Johannes Reissner, "Die Idrīsiden in `Asīr. Ein historischer Überblick," *Die Welt des Islams* XXI (1981), 164-192.

[135]Beehler, *History*, pp. 52, 60.

[136]NRO Darfur 1/3/16.

moment of the Italian invasion, and he asked `Alī Dīnār for continued support: "truly the unbelievers are pouring in everywhere," he wrote grimly; "these days there is not a king on the face of the earth except for you" (Doc. 14). The sultan was authorized to commandeer camels from the Sanūsī settlement at al-Dōr to facilitate emergency transport north (Docs. 15, 16).

Muḥammad `Ābid's letters to `Alī Dīnār (Docs. 15, 16) emphasized the disruptive effect of the Italian invasion upon trade. "The people of the country [here]," he wrote, "are in a state of siege." "The situation in Benghazi has hurt us," he said, "for we have interests there, and in Tripoli. We have not even heard news from there." It was not likely that normal business could resume "until the land's turmoil ends, for now no one gets into or out of it." "At present," he concluded, "there is no way into the country with regard to implements and such things, and [. . .], perfumes, and garments . . . . We are extremely sorry about the holding up of business there, and about this blockage of the roads" (Doc. 15). In view of these difficulties, Muḥammad `Ābid turned to two local merchants and asked them to obtain as much ammunition for `Alī Dīnār's ivory as they could from the stocks of other merchants in Kufra itself; these transactions, the "big sale in Kufra" of Document 15, were carried out between the arrival of the ivory on 21 December 1911 and the preparation of the register alluded to (Doc. 15) on 15 January 1912.[137] The surviving register fragments indicate that Ḥammad Bū Kāda sold four *aṭrāf* (*qinṭārs*) of *dhufākhira* (high quality) ivory weigning 59 (*raṭls*?) at a rate of 137.5 (rounds of ammunition) per (*raṭl*?), yielding 8,113 rounds. Al-Ḥājj `Īsā b. `Uwaytha sold one *ṭarf* weighing 10.5 at the same rate, yielding 1,444 rounds. Ḥammad Bū Kāda disposed of an additional *ṭarf* of "split Sudanese" (*Sūdānī mashqūq*) weighing 8.5 at a rate of 100, yielding an additional 850 rounds. In sum, six of the *qinṭārs* of `Alī Dīnār's ivory delivered by Faraj Khalīfa were sold for 10,407 rounds of Greek (Doc. 15) ammunition; these were placed in storage in the house of al-Ḥājj `Alī Qarjayla al-Majābrī (Doc. 26). In view of future events, it is important to note that the bulk of this ammunition was not, in fact, sent to the Sudan. The register fragments seem to suggest that Muḥammad

[137]Fragments of this document survive but have not been included in this book; the words cited are transliterated precisely from the spelling of the fragments.

Ābid regarded at least 6,000 rounds as compensation for ammunition sent south previously; `Alī Dīnār, in contrast, expected payment in full (Doc. 30).

The close of 1911 brought another misfortune to Kufra in the form of the death on 3 September of Aḥmad al-Rīfī, distinguished elder statesman of the brotherhood and the last surviving personal companion of the Grand Sanūsī (Docs. 14, 16). Aḥmad al-Sharīf's account of his passing (Doc. 14) is certainly one of the most moving episodes in the correspondence; in it, he emphasized that the wise old man's spiritual scepter had passed to him, which could not fail to enhance Aḥmad al-Sharīf's own growing reputation for religious authority--even his enemies had begun to call him "The Black Pope." `Alī Dīnār sent currency to Kufra to settle Aḥmad al-Rīfī's estate (Doc. 14); the coins, upon receipt, were handed over to his grandson (Doc. 16).

The documents of January 1912 contained a number of small but illuminating illustrations of the times. Transport camels had been weakened by the cold to the extent that they must be replaced at a financial loss, while others had died. A Sanūsī trader on the Wadai road had been robbed; could `Alī Dīnār please help him? A special effort would be made to procure ammunition for a gun previously sent to al-Fāshir as a present, along with a bandoleer fit for a king. Gifts of horses continued to be exchanged between Kufra and Dār Fūr (Doc. 15). Aḥmad al-Sharīf, who had a longstanding weakness in this regard, asked for three attractive slave girls (Doc. 14).[138] `Alī al-Khaṭṭābī, a more important figure than his role in this correspondence would suggest, thanked the Dār Fūr sultan for the timely gift of a gun (Doc. 17). This proved to be a wise investment in good will on the part of the king, for late in 1915, when the Sanūsī were victorious and `Alī Dīnār's kingdom threatened, `Alī al-Khaṭṭābī would send 600 Mannlicher-Carcano rifles and ammunition south from the Cyrenaican coast to the aid of Dār Fūr.[139]

In May 1911 the French conquered the Ennedi. Ṣāliḥ Abū Karīm fled to Dār Fūr, accompanied by `Abd al-Raḥīm Bū Maṭārī* and "a large number of his followers of the Aulad Sliman and Zueia [Awlād Sulaymān and Zuwayya] and

[138]There survives a letter in which Aḥmad al-Sharīf, as a young man in Gouro in 1901, sent a similar request south to the commander of the *zāwiya* at Bir Alali; see Triaud, *Tchad*, Doc. 10, pp. 107-109.

[139]NRO Darfur 1/3/16. Theobald (*`Alī Dīnār*, p. 160) may refer to this shipment.

about 10,000 Tuareg."[140] The king settled the newcomers at a site near Kabkābiyya significantly called "al-Dōr" and westward toward Kereinik; they then began to raid `Alī Dīnār's subjects, notably the Meidob, and also the distant Kabbābīsh and other groups subject to Khartoum.[141] The sultan was not willing to tolerate this behavior, and during 1912 he cracked down.

> He put Saleh in prison and insisted on disarming them and attempted to seize their slaves for his army and their girls for his 'harim' in addition to demanding taxes. Many of the Tawarek decamped whence they had come; others resisted, and inflicted severe losses upon the Sultan. Finally those that had not fled were subjected and transplanted to the south of Fasher, where they still are [in 1916] . . . . The Senussi [leaders] apparently resented Ali Dinar's treatment of the Tawarek refugees and wrote to him on the subject in strong terms.[142]

Document 18, dated 22 September 1912, is a letter in strong terms from Kufra protesting `Alī Dīnār's treatment of the Tuareg; it was written by Sayyid Idrīs, whom Aḥmad al-Sharīf had left in charge there when he rode north in June 1912 to take personal command at the Cyrenaican front.[143] The letter could not have reached al-Fāshir much before December 1912; when it did, the sultan released Ṣāliḥ Abū Karīm and again expelled him from Dār Fūr, this time courteously, on "an embassy to the Senussi."[144] The mission set out to deliver grain to the beleaguered *zāwiya* of Gouro, but in May 1913 the French waylaid the caravan on its way west to Tibesti; Ṣāliḥ Abū Karīm was captured and carried off to prison in Fort Archambault, while his son and several other Sanūsī notables were killed.[145] The resettled Tuareg of Dār Fūr were allowed one further opportunity to draw their swords against the Christians; as Anglo-Egyptian forces moved to envelop the sultanate late in 1915, a force of about 300 Kinīn were sent to defend a post in the Zaghāwa country.[146]

[140]NRO Darfur 1/3/16.

[141]Ibid.

[142]Ibid.

[143]Ciammaichella, *Libyens et Français*, p. 120.

[144]NRO Darfur 1/3/16.

[145]Ciammaichella, *Libyens et Français*, p. 123; NRO Darfur 1/3/16.

[146]NRO Darfur 1/4/18.

During 1913 famine tightened its grip on the central Sahara and Sudan, and warfare exacted a high toll as the French moved to expell the Sanūsiyya from its last posts in northern Chad. In the north, when the Italo-Turkish peace of October 1912 had removed the Ottomans from the defense of Libya, during 1913 the Sanūsī were left to face the Europeans alone. The following year this struggle was forced into a new and broader context by the outbreak of World War I. Formal contacts between Kufra and al-Fāshir became less frequent during these years (Doc. 23), but caravans bearing `Alī Dīnār's goods still headed north at intervals (Doc. 20), and many private traders from the Sanūsī world continued to visit Dār Fūr. Documents 19, 20, 21 and 22, most undated, seem to originate from this troubled period. With the exception of Document 20 the writers are comparatively obscure individuals or unknown, though on the evidence of their contents the letters clearly derive from the Sanūsī world. The messages they bore were often dramatic, but sometimes vague, and the present authors have not always been able to understand them; `Alī Dīnār would have faced similar problems of interpretation when they reached his hands.

Document 19, written in the eastern script characteristic of Dār Fūr rather than the Maghribī hand of official Sanūsī correspondence, appears to be a fragment of a spy's report to `Alī Dīnār on the activities of Sanūsī merchants. It reported the arrival in al-Fāshir of Sanūsī traders from French-occupied Wadai, (a road until recently closed by the sultan's embargo),[147] and it distinguished between the Dār Fūr based party of Abū Bakr al-Ghadāmsī and a second group, presumably of northern origin, led by "Ghayth," possibly Ghayth Abū Karīm or Ghayth Abū Qandīl of previous mention. One is told that when the northern merchants reached Dār Tāma bearing guns and ammunition intended as a present for `Alī Dīnār as well as their own wares, the sultan of Dār Tāma, "the Tāmāwī" in Sudanese idiom, exercised his traditional kingly prerogative and took for himself the items appropriate to royalty. But this Tāma sultan, Ḥasan b. Ya`qūb b. Ibrāhīm (reigned 1910-1920), was an appointee and puppet of the French commander at Abesher; "the Christian" seems to have heeded the merchants' appeal, and "paid them compensation out of his own treasury."[148] Of the

[147] `Alī Dīnār forbade trade with Wadai for three years following the fall of Abesher; see Kapteijns, *Mahdist Faith*, p. 195.

[148] Kapteijns and Spaulding, *After the Millennium*, p. xvi; Docs. 38-40, pp. 211-223.

present for `Alī Dīnār, however, only a few rounds of ammunition remained. From the distant Mediterranean front came news which, south of the Sahara, was being interpreted as a great victory for the forces of Islam; `Alī Dīnār was told that the Italians had been forced to pay sixteen million pounds to the Ottomans and the Sanūsiyya in return for a truce. This was probably a very garbled reference to Article X of the Treaty of Lausanne, which ended the Italo-Turkish War in October 1912; the Italians did undertake to pay the Turks a large sum, but not because they were defeated--rather, as a form of compensation for the abrogation of Ottoman claims to Libya.[149]

Document 20 is an undated letter to `Alī Dīnār from Muḥammad Hilāl in Kufra, bearing the seal of Aḥmad al-Sharīf, who had left the oasis for the Mediterranean front in June 1912. The letter acknowledged the arrival of a consignment of the sultan's ivory and ostrich feathers, promising to arrange their exchange for guns and ammunition as soon as this was possible. Muḥammad Hilāl thanked the sultan for sending the three slave girls requested previously by his brother (Doc. 14), and arranged to send the sultan a kingly array of luxurious clothing, horse trappings and household furnishings--as recorded "in the manifest in the possession of brother Khalīl"--but no munitions.[150] The tone of the letter is conspicuously cooler than its counterparts from earlier years, perhaps largely because of Sanūsī objections to `Alī Dīnār's forceful suppression of Ṣāliḥ Abū Karīm's turbulent Tuareg refugees during 1912 (Doc. 18). Kufra now decided to disband the Sanūsī command of al-Dōr; as Muḥammad Hilāl put it, "The intention is to ease [things] for you and for others." Sanūsī livestock was to be removed to Kufra

[149]Beehler, *History*, p. 100. News of this treaty could probably not have reached al-Fāshir much before the end of the year but would not have remained newsworthy much later, which suggests that Document 19 was probably written in early 1913.

[150]A very imperfect copy of the manifest of goods delivered to `Alī Dīnār by Khalīl has survived, and it suffices to establish the absence of munitions and the general character of the items sent. The present authors believe, however, that the modern copyist in Khartoum did not fully understand many of the western names for turn-of-the-century imported trade goods, so that any attempt to reconstruct the list on the basis of his draft would be too speculative to serve any useful purpose.

or even Cyrenaica--clearly an extreme measure--while the *ikhwān* of al-Dōr had been ordered to make their way "to the region of Kalaka." The latter command strongly suggests that the letter was written before the fall of `Ayn Galakka to the French in November 1913.

Document 21 is an undated letter to `Alī Dīnār from a Sanūsī partisan named Muḥammad al-Shaykh Makki b. `Abd Allāh b. Ṣāliḥ Ruz,* who wrote to thank the king for generous assistance to those of his kinsmen who had fled the European advance to seek refuge in Dār Fūr. The letter provides a wholesome corrective to the drama of the fall of Ṣāliḥ Abū Karīm and his Tuareg; peacefully-inclined refugees were welcomed in Dār Fūr and had every reason to be grateful to `Alī Dīnār. The present authors have not been able to identify Shaykh Muḥammad and his people, nor al-Ruz, with certainty. Since Shaykh Muḥammad referred to Gouro as being "in the Sudan," or south of the desert, and since he thanked the king for opening a road by which he and his masters, in case of need, could go south, it is probable that he was Libyan. Since he correctly foresaw the impending fall of Gouro to the Europeans, it is probable that he wrote toward the end of 1913--the French entered Gouro on 14 December. However, Shaykh Muḥammad did not distinguish between European nations; to him, all the intruders from north or south were "Italians" who, at the time of his writing, not only threatened Gouro but had "arisen from all places, [from] Tripoli and Benghazi," and now stood at the border of his homeland, al-Ruz. To which Italian advance could Shaykh Muḥammad's letter refer? Since most of the Mediterranean front was locked in stalemate throughout 1913, Shaykh Muḥammad's portrayal of his people as victims of an impressive Italian attack is most easily to be understood in the context of one exceptional situation--the Italian invasion of the Fazzān. Colonel Miani struck south from the Sirtican coast in early August and by the middle of December had reached Brak, having encountered heavy resistance south of Soqna as he entered lands loyal to the Sanūsiyya. Perhaps Shaykh Muḥammad and his people were among those who stood astride his column's line of march. Miani pressed on to occupy Murzūq, the capital of the Fazzān, on 3 March 1914.[151]

[151] Ambrogio Bollati, *Enciclopedia dei nostri combattimenti coloniale fino al 2 Ottobre 1935-xiii* (Torino: Giulio Einaudi, 1936-xiiii), pp. 136, 171-173. For the arrival in al-Fāshir of refugees from the Fazzān, see NRO Darfur 1/3/16.

Document 22 is a letter of 20 November 1914 to `Alī Dīnār from `Abd al-Raḥīm Maṭārī, a commander in Sanūsī service and former associate of Ṣāliḥ Abū Karīm (Doc. 18), who had traveled widely and now sought good relations with the sultan in order to return to Dār Fūr--in which attempt he had experienced many misadventures. Of the several newsworthy events of 1914 communicated in this letter, the most momentuous was the outbreak of World War I, news of which had probably reached `Alī Dīnār through other channels within a week of its outbreak.[152] `Abd al-Raḥīm understood the conflict to be a fight against the English on the part of Aḥmad al-Sharīf, the Ottomans and the Germans, and though the foreign protagonists had done little as yet, Aḥmad al-Sharīf had scored an impressive success in winning the loyalty and support of the oasis community of Siwa, which lay east of Jaghbūb in territory subject to British-dominated Egypt. Soldiers recruited at Siwa had taken up positions with the Sanūsī forces threatening the port of al-Salūm, historically a part of Cyrenaica but ceded to Egypt by the Ottomans late in 1911 to prevent its capture by the Italians; the port would be occupied in turn by the Sanūsiyya and the British during 1915 and 1916.[153]

Italy did not formally join World War I for six months after `Abd al-Raḥīm's letter, but hostilities had already been underway in the Libyan theater since 1911, and she was the major opponent of the Sanūsiyya there throughout. `Abd al-Raḥīm belatedly reported the arrival in the north of Aḥmad al-Sharīf (June 1912), along with Idrīs, (who soon withdrew from the conflict into eastern exile). During the summer of 1914 Aḥmad al-Sharīf assigned his youngest brother Ṣafī al-Dīn the task of reorganizing and broadening the anti-Italian forces in Tripolitania, where Miani's long march south to Murzūq had been possible only because the invaders had struck an alliance of convenience with the Sirtican chieftain Sayf al-Naṣr*[154] Sayf al-Naṣr was soon won over secretly to the Sanūsī side, but encouraged to bide his time. The letter

[152]For example, Anglo-Egyptian intelligence in northern Kordofan intercepted a letter to the sultan to this effect written on 3 August 1914; see Theobald, *`Alī Dīnār*, p. 137.

[153]Evans-Pritchard, *The Sanusi*, pp. 125-128.

[154]Bollati, *Enciclopedia*, p. 172.

of `Abd al-Raḥīm mentioned a clash between Sayf al-Naṣr and an Italian identified as "Kūnus," possibly an officer named Cassinis who commanded on the Sirtican front at that time. The clash may be the incident recorded by the Italians as the action of Wādī al-Aḥmar, fought in the Sirtica on 7 July 1914, in which there were eight Italian casualties.[155] Following the fight Ṣafī al-Dīn attempted to see whether the truce between Sayf al-Naṣr and "Kūnus" still held. Meanwhile, `Abd al-Raḥīm reported, Muḥammad `Ābid had left Kufra and gone west to the Fazzān (in August 1914)[156] to help organize the resistance, and open fighting broke out on the twenty-sixth of that month.[157] As the year lengthened Miani found himself increasingly isolated and greatly overextended in Murzūq as accelerating Sanūsī raids interrupted his long and tenuous lines of supply and communication to the coast. On 6 November his superiors in Tripoli ordered him to fall back on Brak, the administrative center of the district of al-Shiyāṭī to which, as `Abd al-Raḥīm reported, Muḥammad `Ābid pursued him. (Miani and the survivors of his column eventually reached safety at the coast on Christmas day). The author of Document 22, writing on 20 November 1914, could not have anticipated the succession of Sanūsī victories in western Libya that followed,[158] as a result of which, by next May, "Sayyid Safi al-Din marched into Old Tripolitania to put himself, in the name of the Sanusiya, at the head of the Arab resistance."[159]

As war clouds gathered at the close of 1914 `Alī Dīnār became increasingly concerned about the fate of the arms and ammunition he had purchased from Kufra (Docs. 15, 16, 20), but which had never been delivered to Dār Fūr. Documents 23 through 30, embracing the last year and a half of the history of the Dār Fūr sultanate, all focus upon the collection of this debt; though the sultan remained loyal to the Sanūsī alliance, he expressed increasing exasperation with Muḥammad `Ābid, whom he regarded as personally responsible for the long

[155]Bollati, *Enciclopedia*, p. 235.

[156]Evans-Pritchard, *The Sanusi*, p. 122.

[157]Bollati, *Enciclopedia*, p. 157.

[158]Ibid., pp. 210 (Sebha, 27-28 November), 165 (Bu Ngem, early December) and 180-181 (Qasr Bu Hadi, 27-28 April 1915).

[159]Evans-Pritchard, *The Sanusi*, p. 122.

delay in the delivery of his munitions. The arms were badly needed, for `Alī Dīnār's relations with the Anglo-Egyptian authorities in Khartoum were rapidly deteriorating. Perhaps he sensed that the British had proposed the annexation of his kingdom as early as 1913, and with the outbreak of World War I he found his formal subordination to a non-Islamic power intolerable; in December 1914 he accused the masters of the Nile valley of distorting Islam, by March 1915 he was convinced that the British intended to attack him, and in April he renounced his tributary relationship to Khartoum. Late in July 1915 the Anglo-Egyptian authorities decided to occupy Dār Fūr, and began to lay plans for the conquest.[160] The last contacts between Kufra and al-Fāshir would be closely monitored by spies.

"It is a long time since we received any news from you," wrote `Alī Dīnār to Aḥmad al-Sharīf, sometime in 1333/1914-1915, "which we believe is due to pressure of work in the cause of the Jehad for the sake of God" (Doc. 23). Indeed, there was ample reason for difficulty in communication during this Islamic year, for in addition to the distractions of the Sanūsī campaigns against the British at the Egyptian border and against the Italians in western Libya, the normal routes of passage south from Kufra to Dār Fūr had been rendered hazardous by raiding and war ever since the fall of `Ayn Galakka to the French at the close of 1913, as the invaders and the Sanūsiyya struggled bitterly for definitive control over the Teda and Beri-speaking pastoral peoples of northern Chad.[161]

During the later months of 1914 `Alī Dīnār took the initiative in reestablishing contact with Kufra, dispatching as his special envoy the veteran Sanūsī trader Ghayth Abū Karīm, who arrived in Kufra on 19 November (Doc. 25). To secure the flow of commerce the king opened a new road far to the east of the troubles in Chad; it led northeast from al-Fāshir down the Forty Days' Road to Jabal Meidob ("Mīrū"*)[162] and north to the oasis of Nukhayla (Merga)

[160]Theobald, *`Alī Dīnār*, pp. 121-147.

[161]NRO Darfur 1/3/16.

[162]See the discussion of Document 29 below.

before veering northwest toward Libya.[163] Document 24, dated 8 April 1915, is a letter to `Alī Dīnār specifically to express appreciation for the opening of the new road on the part of "all the Majābra [Jalo merchants] residing in Kufra;" similar gratitude was also extended by the Zuwayya trading community in a later letter (Doc. 28).

The mission of Ghayth Abū Karīm to Kufra in November 1914, as reported to Anglo-Egyptian intelligence, was to collect the 10,000 rounds of ammunition owed him for the last three years by Muḥammad `Ābid; the latter, however, "put him off with excuses, and said he had not yet been able to procure the ammunition, etc. etc."[164] This is amply confirmed by the emissary's own report to the king, written on 10 April 1915 (Doc. 26). Muḥammad `Ābid was in no position to forward the 10,000 rounds to Dār Fūr, Ghayth said, because he had taken them west to war during August 1914; in effect, Miani had been expelled from the Fazzān with `Alī Dīnār's bullets. Ghayth added the significant detail that in order for Muḥammad `Ābid to lay hands on the king's ammunition, he had been obliged to drive away the man in whose house it had been left for safekeeping. Some of the people of Kufra may well have objected to such highhanded behavior, (the Zuwayya were to rise against Muḥammad `Ābid and expell him from the oasis a decade later),[165] and it seems likely that such were the individuals, otherwise unknown, who prepared their own letter to `Alī Dīnār (Doc. 25) confirming the substance of Ghayth's account. Meanwhile the envoy waited patiently, his provisions exhausted through months of delay, "incurring debts with people in order to eat" (Doc. 26). Something had to be done.

In July 1915 `Alī Dīnār took a step which, on the evidence of the correspondence considered here, was unprecedented; he sent to Kufra his own

[163]Anglo-Egyptian spies believed that Ghayth went north over the troubled western roads, and that the new route was not opened until June 1915 (NRO Darfur 1/3/16). The former may be true, but the latter is not, for Documents 24 and 25, written in Kufra in April 1915, already express gratitude to the king for the new access to his country. It would therefore seem plausible that the spies erred, and that the king's new messenger at the close of 1914 also opened his new road.

[164]NRO Darfur 1/3/16.

[165]Evans-Pritchard, *The Sanusi*, p. 187.

royal caravan. The commander was the Wadaian exile nobleman Aḥmad, Dūd Murra's *'aqīd al-Zabāda*, who had served `Alī Dīnār faithfully since his flight to Dār Fūr in 1910. The *'aqīd* probably bore the original letter of which Document 23 is a translation, and he was accompanied by an impressive escort comprised of a mounted squadron of about thirty of `Alī Dīnār's military slaves and a hundred warriors from among the Dār Fūr Tuareg, as well as many private merchants and several hundred camels--some gifts to the Sanūsiyya, others to be exchanged for arms in Kufra. Nothing quite like this had ever been seen in the desert north of Dār Fūr; Anglo-Egyptian spies filed long reports and French agents in Chad took the trouble to warn the British in Kordofan (via diplomatic cable routed from Abesher to Brazzaville, Paris, Cairo, Khartoum and al-Nahūd) that "the sultan of Dar Fur has sent mounted soldiers to hasten the arrival of arms and ammunition from Kufra, for which our irregular cavalry detachments are on the lookout."[166]

The *'aqīd* Aḥmad reached Kufra after a difficult journey; many camels died (Doc. 27), though the escort arrived at the oasis (and later returned to Dār Fūr) safely (Doc. 29). After a stay of about two months in the oasis, by early November the *'aqīd*, assisted by Ghayth the unfortunate emissary, had made some purchases of arms and organized a caravan to return to al-Fāshir. They had not succeeded in collecting the 10,000 rounds of ammunition owed to their king, but they did bring a letter from Muḥammad `Ābid conveying an optimistic appraisal of the course of the war in the north (Doc. 27), and were accompanied on the road south by a party of Zuwayya merchants from the oasis who bore their own letter of introduction to the king (Doc. 28).

The return march of the *'aqīd's* caravan to Dār Fūr was very difficult. The men "suffered a great deal from want of water, for they could not get any except every seven or eight days, and they arrived in a very bad state of fatigue," Anglo-Egyptian spies reported, while only about thirty of the 200 camels that had left Kufra reached al-Fāshir.[167] Couriers bore news of the misfortune

[166]Several accounts of the expedition, including a subsequent interview with the *'aqīd* Aḥmad himself and a translation of the French message cited, may be found in NRO Darfur 1/3/16.

[167]NRO Darfur 1/3/16.

quickly to the king, who sent out a support caravan of fresh camels with water and provisions to intercept and relieve the approaching expedition. The rendezvouz, believed by the spies to have taken place at Bīr Naṭrūn, was successful. It would seem that the *`aqīd* and his escort returned quickly and unobtrusively to the capital with the relief caravan, while Ghayth led the surviving camels of the main caravan and the private merchants from Kufra slowly on to Jabal Meidob. At their arrival there on 24 December 1915, they fell under the direct scrutiny of Anglo-Egyptian agents. "They sent Ibrahim El Haj [ahead to al-Fāshir] to give the information of their arrival," the spies reported, and he probably also delivered to the king Document 27, written by Ghayth at Jabal Mīrū (thus meaning Jabal Meidob) to introduce the party. In response, according to the spies, "the sultan sent Gumaa wad Gadein El Ziadi to meet and entertain them, and gave orders that Gheis should enter El Fasher on the 28th of Dec., and on Friday the 31st, which is the parade day, he will receive him [officially]."[168] The royal reception took place on schedule, and two weeks later `Alī Dīnār would claim that Ghayth had just brought him 2,500 Mauser rifles and 400 cases of ammunition.[169] Spies suggested, however, that only about 400 weapons were actually delivered.

On 29 January 1916 `Alī Dīnār wrote Document 30, addressed to Aḥmad al-Sharīf, whom he congratulated upon Sanūsī military successes. However, he also appealed for redress in regard to the ammunition that had never been sent in return for his ivory, and he criticized Muḥammad `Ābid sharply. Finally, he wrote that the Muslims of the eastern Sudan had become Christians under British rule; while this was not true, the king was not wrong in his perception that his eastern neighbors had become enemies, for preparations were already underway in Khartoum for the Anglo-Egyptian invasion of Dār Fūr that followed in March 1916. Condominium troops entered al-Fāshir on 23 May, and the restored Dār Fūr sultanate of `Alī Dīnār was at an end. The king himself fought on; he was run to earth and killed on 5 November 1916.

[168]NRO Darfur 1/3/16.

[169]Theobald, *`Alī Dīnār*, p. 162.

At the fall of al-Fāshir on 23 May 1916 the conquerors found that on the whole "Ali Dinar's clerical staff were a surprisingly efficient body . . . . there was of course no filing system but [the head clerk] could usually ferret out from some closet a record which was neatly written and well kept up to date."[170] On the other hand, the intelligence agent H.A. MacMichael reported that "much looting went on, especially at the palace, before the guards could be put in,"[171] and he spent most of the next month sifting through heaps of rubbish left behind by the palace looters to collect bags and boxes of the sultan's records for shipment to the central archives in Khartoum.[172] MacMichael's gleanings, lightly organized, may be found today in the Sudanese National Records Office (NRO), in the files of the Intelligence Department of the Condominium era. The first professional historian to work with this material characterized one sequence of files as "a miscellaneous mass of letters and intelligence reports, in no chronological order" and a second as "scattered papers concerning Ali Dinar."[173] The documents offered here may be found in those two omnibus files: NRO Intelligence 5/3/40 "Papers concerning Ali Dinar" and NRO Intelligence 2/3/12 "Ali Dinar Historical."

There was to be a small but revealing epilogue to the story of the Islamic alliance between `Alī Dīnār and the Sanūsiyya. In the north the Italian colonial enterprise took on renewed vigor with the rise of Fascism, and by the end of 1928 Italian motorized columns were poised to strike into the desert fastnesses of southern Libya. Muḥammad `Ābid was recalled from his recent disgrace to lead Kufra in the hour of need; on his return, he wrote at once a letter appealing for supplies of grain and sheep to Muḥammad Baḥr al-Dīn, current pretender to the throne of Dār Fūr. The prince dutifully turned the letter over to the British Resident who now occupied `Alī Dīnār's palace in al-Fāshir. Kufra fell to the Italians on 20 January 1931.[174]

[170]J.A. Gillan, "Darfur 1916," *Sudan Notes and Records* XXII, 1 (1939), 18.

[171]Theobald, *'Ali Dinar*, p. 193.

[172]Kapteijns and Spaulding, *After the Millennium*, p. 5.

[173]Theobald, *'Ali Dinar*, p. 226.

[174]Bollati, *Enciclopedia*, pp. 288-292.

DOCUMENTS

DOCUMENT 1

When the Sanūsī leadership resolved upon a program of expansive activities into the southlands and al-Mahdī brought the seat of the brotherhood first to Kufra and then to Gouro, it was natural for the order to devote considerable attention to the collapse of the Mahdist state in the Sudan and to `Alī Dīnār's restoration of the Dār Fūr sultanate. The first Sanūsī mission to the new kingdom was well received in 1899, and further contacts followed. It was said that the young sultan had accepted induction into the order; one *zāwiya* was established at his capital in al-Fāshir, while the formation of a second was authorized pending the selection of a suitable site, and correspondence passed back and forth along the newly established line of communication.[1]

The first document in the present collection is a list of presents sent by `Alī Dīnār to the incumbent head of the Sanūsī brotherhood. Though undated, it may be placed chronologically within the interval between the first Sanūsī mission to Dār Fūr (which returned to Gouro in December 1899)[2] and the death of al-Mahdī in early June 1902. The gifts were generous, and one may speculate that they perhaps reflected the unclouded enthusiasm of first contact. The goods sent to Gouro were largely luxury consumption items appropriate to the life-style of the Sudanese elite; noteworthy was the absence of both the weapons ("instruments of state," in the idiom of the day) that would have figured prominently in comparable gifts to a secular ruler and the ivory that formed the basis of subsequent commercial exchanges. One may suggest that at this early stage of his relationship to the Sanūsiyya `Alī Dīnār esteemed the brotherhood primarily for its religious merits. As indicated above in the introduction, events in Wadai were soon to disillusion the king, precipitating an extended break in his ties to the brotherhood; when the relationship was restored, it would rest on a somewhat less idealistic basis.

Present understanding of `Alī Dīnār's chancery suggests that "while incoming letters, tax records and the like were kept at court, outgoing correspondence was not copied and stored."[3] It would seem, however, that the court did keep lists of the valuables sent abroad with caravans; the document considered here is but one of several that have survived from `Alī Dīnār's reign.[4]

(. . .)[5] سيدنا واستاذنا السيد محمد المهدي ابن السيد علي السنوسي الشريف

الحسني الخطابي رضي الله عنه /

(. . .)ه [5] /

عدد /

طاقتين تيل ابيض عال العال /

ثلاثه طاقاة دبلان ابو شيشه عال العال /

ثلاثه طاقات دبلان نمر سبعه عال /

طاقتين دبلان محضي بزيق بالطرفين /

سته طاقاة مرمر ابيض ثقيل سبعه كوارته /

سته طاقاة مرمر ابيض خفيف /

ثلاثه ثياب كشمير صوف ابيض متركش باطرافه /

ملافح لزوم ردا بيوض محضيات /

سته تياب سلك الفضه ناعمين لزوم قطا /

ثلثماية ريال مجيدي جيد /

قنطار صابون مصري نابلسي /

قداحه زرق خشبه لزوم الطعام /

مناديل حمر لزوم وضع القداحه عليهم /

براتيل حمر لزوم قطا القداحه ⁄

حمار ريناوي ابيض اللون شامي طويل التابه مكلف بكامل العده ⁄

واحد بتل مكادي بسرجه ⁄

بروش اثنان لزوم الصلا واحد ابيض وواحد احمر لهم رقاب ⁄

بروش مفارش اثنين حمر عال العال ⁄

(. . . .) ذراع (. . .) [5] ⁄

فرك برصه حرير بالولادهم [6] ثلاثه حرير ⁄

ثياب دوريه سواكني ⁄

فرك حرير زرق ⁄

جوز مخدات قطن باكياس عليهم تنتنه بالطرافهم [6] ⁄

عنتريب لولب ⁄

لحاف قطن مقشيا بشية ⁄

ثوبين لزوم قطا عنتريب واحده قطني وواحده مرمر عليهم حضاياة جاوه حمره وتنتنه ⁄

واحده ليانه خيط ملونه بخضار وصفار وبياض ⁄

واحده ناموسيه عال مرمر مجوزه داخلها شية مكشكشه بالطرافها [6] بحمار تنتنه ⁄

رشمه فضه مصريه بشريط مقصب وجدله لزوم الحمار

(To)[7] our lord and our teacher, al-Sayyid Muḥammad al-Mahdī, son of al-Sayyid `Alī al-Sanūsī, al-Sharīf al-Ḥasanī al-Khaṭṭābī, May God be pleased with him.

[...] [5]

Number:

Two rolls[8] of top quality[9] white linen.[10]

Three rolls of top quality calico[11] "With The Water Pipe."[12]

Three rolls of good quality [13] calico "Number Seven."[14]

Two rolls of pure calico with a border on both edges.

Six rolls of heavy white *marmar*[14] "Seven Rings."[15]

Six rolls of light white *marmar*.

Three white Kashmir woolen robes with ornamented borders.[16]

Pure white *malḥaf*s[17] for use as cloaks.[18]

Six soft robes with silver thread for use as covers.[19]

Three hundred *Majīdī* dollars,[20] of good quality.[21]

A *qinṭār*[22] of Egyptian Nāblus-style[23] soap.

Dark wooden bowls to use for food.

Red napkins[24] upon which to place the bowls.

Colored food-covers[25] with which to cover[26] the bowls.

An Upper-Egyptian[27] donkey, white in color, of Syrian breed, tall of stature, equipped with complete trappings.

One Abyssianian mule,[28] with its saddle.

Two mats for use in prayer, one plain and one colored, with necks.[29]

Two colored mats for furnishing, of top quality.

[... cubits...].[30]

Women's wrappers[31] of Bursa silk, with three matching scarves.[32]

Robes native to[33] Suakin.

Woman's wrappers of blue silk.

A pair of cotton cushions with pillow-cases bordered with lace.[34]

A bed with springs.[35]

A cotton bed cover of printed calico.[36]

Two cloths[37] for use in covering[38] a bed, one of cotton and one of *marmar*, [each] with borders[39] of red *jāwa* cloth.[40]

One bed sheet,[41] colored with green, yellow and white thread.

One mosquito net of good quality doubled *marmar*, its inside edges of printed calico pleated with decorative cloth [42] and lace.

A silver Egyptian donkey halter with brocaded strap and noseband.[43]

1. Triaud, "Relations, pp. 844-846.

2. Ibid., p. 844.

3. O'Fahey and Abu Salim, *Land in Dār Fūr*, p. 23.

4. See above, Introduction; Kapteijns and Spaulding, "Gifts Worthy of Kings," and Kapteijns and Spaulding, *After the Millennium*, Document 74, pp. 368-371.

5. Lacuna.

6. Spelled as shown.

7. Lacuna, conjectural reading. The summary English translation which the British colonial administration attached confirms this reading.

8. *Ṭāqa*: a complete *thawb*, rolled (*malfūf*) (`Awn al-Sharīf Qāsim, *Al-Lahja al-`Ammiyya fi'l-Sūdān* (Khartoum: Al-Dār al-Sūdāniyya li'l-Kutub, 1972), p. 486); "*Pièce d'étoffe*" (R.P.A. Dozy, *Supplément aux Dictionnaires Arabes* (Beirut: Librairie du Liban, 1968), II, p. 71).

9. *`Āl-al-`āl*: the best of the best.

10. *Tīl*: linen (Hans Wehr, *A Dictionary of Modern Written Arabic*. Edited by J. Milton Cowan (Wiesbaden: Otto Harrassowitz, 1971), p. 100 and `Awn, *Al-Lahja*, p.107); Dozy, *Supplément*, I, p. 156: (silk piping).

11. *Dubbalān* is calico. See H.F.S. Amery, *English-Arabic Vocabulary for the Use of Officials in the Anglo-Egyptian Sudan* (Cairo: Al-Mokattam Printing Office, 1905), p. 55 (Dablān), S. Hillelson, *Sudan Arabic English-Arabic Vocabulary* (London: Sudan Government, 1925), p. 45 (dabelān), and `Awn, *Al-Lahja*, p. 224 (a variety of cotton cloth).

12. Probably the cloth bore the trade-mark of a waterpipe.

13. *`Āl*: of good quality. Contrast note 3 above.

14. A kind of cloth. We have not been able to identify this term.

15. Probably the cloth bore the trade-mark of seven rings.

16. Conjectural reading. Possibly a variation of the root *raqasha*, which in its second form means "to embellish, to adorn."

17. An extended description of the use of the *malḥaf* in Dār Fūr is given by Le Cheikh Mohammed Ebn-Omar El Tounsy, *Voyage au Ouadây* (Paris: Benjamin Duprat, 1851) p. 58: "le *malhaf* est une grande pièce d'étoffe que les Fôriens de la classe aisée se jettent à plusieurs tours sur les épaules en manière de baudrier, et qui a la forme et l'apparence des *milâjéh* d'Egypte. Le *malhaf* est en mousseline, ou bien en *ilâdjéh* ou *ilâguéh* (étoffe de Syrie, d'un

tissu assez fort, en soie et coton, avec des petits dessins en soie comme brochés) mais toujours avec de longues franges. On s'en drape en sautoir redoublé ci-à-di sur les deaux épaules, comme je viens de l'indiquer, ou bien en cercle tombant de la nuque sur le devant de la poitrine, les bouts rejetés par derrière le dos. Lorsque quelqu'un, vêtu du *malhaf*, paraît devant le sultan, il met aussitôt en ceinture; c'est une règle de bienséance et de décorum."

18. Wehr, *A Dictionary*, p. 336. The term *arday* for "cloak" was commonly used in Libya and in the Sudan trade (Anthony Cachia, *Libya under the Second Ottoman Occupation (1835-1911)* (Tripoli: Government Press, 1945), p. 118).

19. Reading *ghuṭā'* for *quṭā*; the *ghuṭā'* is a "voile, grand voile de femme qui couvre la tete et le corps tout entier" (Dozy, *Supplément*, II, p. 217). See also Wehr, *A Dictionary*, p. 677, and `Awn, *Al-Lahja*, p. 556, who suggest the more general meaning of "covering" or "wrapping." Historically, Sudanese women have not worn the *ghuṭā'* and the term is not widely used there.

20. The *Majīdī* dollar or *riyāl Majīdī* was a silver Ottoman coin worth one-fifth of a Turkish golden pound, or twenty piasters. It was introduced by Sultan `Abd al-Majīd (1839-1861).

21. *Jayyid*, as applied to coins, means unclipped and unblemished by wear. Northeast African users were often very sensitive to even minor deformities in coins, which when present substantially reduced their value.

22. An Egyptian *qinṭār* of the early twentieth century weighed 44.928 kg; the contemporary *qinṭār* of Tripoli weighed 51.282 kg.

23. This seems the most probable meaning of the adjectives "Egyptian Nāblūsī." The Palestinian soap industry rose to regional prominence during the nineteenth century.

24. *Manādīl* are normally handkerchiefs, but here the context suggests the translation "napkins."

25. The *bartāl* or *tabaq* is a decorative food cover of plaited fibre (`Awn, *Al-Lahja*, p. 35), for which the court of al-Fāshir was famous.

26. Reading *ghuṭā'* for *quṭā*; the context suggests the general meaning "to cover."

27. *Rīfāwī*: the donkeys of Upper-Egypt were highly esteemed.

28. Reading *baghl* for *baql*.

29. Prayer mats were often made with a protruding extension on one side, to which the worshiper would touch the forehead during prostration. Prayer mats of this kind are still common in Sudan.

30. Damage to the paper prevents the reading of one entry here.

31. `Awn, *Al Lahja*, p. 577. For a discussion of *firka*, see D. Griselda el-Tayib, "Women's Dress in the Northern Sudan," in *The Sudanese Woman*, ed. Susan Kenyon (London: Ithaca Press, 1987), p. 48.

32. This is how we interpret *bi-awlādihim*.

33. Conjectural translation.

34. `Awn, *Al-Lahja*, p. 100 defines *tantana* as " a form of embellishment at the borders." J. Spencer Trimingham, *Sudan Colloquial Arabic* (London: Oxford University Press, 2nd ed., 1946), p. 160 gives "lace."

35. For the importance of this gift, compare Kapteijns and Spaulding, *After the Millennium*, pp. 474-475.

36. Reading *mughshiyyā* for *muqshiyyā*. *Shīt* is printed calico (Amery, *English-Arabic*, p. 55; Hillelson, *Sudan Arabic*, p. 45).

37. In the Sudan, *thawb* often refers to a garment; here, however, the context suggests the more general meaning "cloth."

38. See note 20.

39. Conjectural translation.

40. *Jāwa*: "Red cloth used for flags and decorations" (Hillelson, *Sudan Arabic*, p. 56).

41. For *liyāna*, see `Awn, *Al-Lahja*, p. 726.

42. Conjectural reading.

43. `Awn, *Al-Lahja*, pp. 116-117.

DOCUMENT 2

The succession dispute that followed the death of Sultan Muḥammad Yūsuf of Wadai precipitated a rupture in `Alī Dīnār's initially cordial relations with the Sanūsiyya; the break extended from 1902 well into 1905. By the latter year, however, Dūd Murra's consolidation of power in Abesher and Kabbābīsh incursions against the Forty Days' Road to Egypt impelled the Dār Fūr monarch to reconsider, and late in 1905 he took the initiative in restoring commercial relations with Kufra. Meanwhile the Sanūsiyya had organized its nomadic supporters in the south, led by the refugee Tuareg of Damergu, into a separate administrative unit and military command called "the camp" or al-Dōr; the primary task of al-Dōr was to oppose the inexorable northward advance of the new French colonial camel corps up the chain of Sanūsī *zāwiyas* based on the oases of western Chad.[1] The nomadic forces of al-Dōr were based on the seasonally grassy highlands of the Ennedi, and since this comparatively fertile plateau adjoined Dār Fūr proper and fell within `Alī Dīnār's sphere of influence, the Sanūsī leaders in Kufra were eager to see amicable relations between the commanders of al-Dōr and the Dār Fūr sultan. By 1908 `Alī Dīnār and the Sanūsiyya were ready to restore more formal diplomatic relations.

Document 2 was written in Kufra during the last quarter of 1908. It was intended to accompany a southward-bound caravan of November-December led by the Ikaskazan chieftain `Abd al-Qādir al-Azraq.[2] The authorities in Kufra explained that he would be remaining "in the vicinity" of Dār Fūr, meaning in the Ennedi, and they expressed the hope that `Alī Dīnār would treat him kindly, particularly since he brought arms to sell. Furthermore, and probably in response to `Alī Dīnār's invitation, the Sanūsī leaders indicated that their former representative to al-Fāshir, Abū Bakr al-Ghadāmsī, would be returning to Dār Fūr soon.

بسم الله الرحمن الرحيم وصلى الله على سيدنا محمد وءاله وصحبه وسلم / فمن العبد الضعيف عبد ربه محمد عابد الشريف الى الملك المعظم السلطان المفخم سلطاننا السلطان / على دينار ابقاه الله تعالى متسنما غوارب المجد متنسما نسائم المدح والحمد ءامين بعد اهداء السلام نرجوا / الله ان لا تنقطع عنى عرائضكم على الدوام فنعرفكم ان راعينا وخديمنا الشيخ عبد القادر الازرق قد اتصلت / بما عنده من الحضرة الي قد استلمت منه ١٠٠ ريال مجيدي عين والاشياء التى بموجب الكشف من / سمن وعسل وجلد وغير ذالك فوالله انى عاجز عن مكافاتكم وكلها جاءت فوق الغاية اسررنا غايت / ما يكون بها ووصلت الينا جميعها سالمة لله الحمد ومن عادة العلماء اذا عجزوا عن المكافات لاحبابهم / يتخذون المساجد دارا والدعاء شعارا نعيالنا محمد الشريف ابنكم واخوته مسلمون عليكم فرحون بما اتاهم / منكم بارك الله فيكم وشكر سعيكم وتقبل عملكم فكل حاجة احسن من الاخرى لاكن اتعبناكم سامحونا / وحين نروا المحل واحد والمحبة الاكيدة التى لا تنفك ما دمت حيا ان شاء الله نرجوا الله ان يتمم / ذالك بالاجتماع ءامين ءامين انه القادر على ذالك وايضا بلغ سلامكم لنا ووصاياتكم جميعها من دلائل الخير / والوصية الخيرية فمقبولة وعلى الراس موضوعة وهى عادتكم ودابكم معنا بحول الله وها هو سفرناه (الاخ)[3] / الشيخ عبد القادر الازرق ياتيكم ان شاء الله تجتمعون به وانتم بخير واوصيناه وحرضنا عليه ان يقيم بابلنا بقرب / بلدانكم وان يكون نظركم فوقه كما هو الظن بكم ما نوصوكم عليه وعنده بعض مصالح اوصيناه يقضيها / من طرفكم الابهى وسلاح يبيعه هناك ويقدم بخير وكان القصد ان يصلكم معه ابى بكر القداسى لاكنه / ما زال ما قدم وان شاء الله ياتيكم حسب امركم ويحكى لكم شفاها ان شاء الله حاصل هذا اليكم وانتم فى عز ودرجة / عالية وقولنا بقرب محلاتكم يقيم ليكن واسطة بيننا وبينكم يصل اليكم

بالجوابات ويرجع ويقضى الحاجة بل / انتم الذين تقضون لنا وله الحاجة فسفروه لنا
عاجلا وقبله ابن الجميع فرج نرجوا الله انه قريب منا وعرفونا بما / يلزم جزاكم الله خيرا
المحل لكم والله يجمعنا بكم عاجلا وان شاء الله نحرضوا التجار ونكاتبوهم ياتوا بالسلاح
يتصدون / بلدتكم البهية صانها رب البرية وانصحونا واخبرونا وبكل شيء عرفونا كما
هى دابكم معنا ابقاكم الله لنا هذا وانى / اطلب الله لكم العفو والعافية والعز والملك
الابدى وعزة الاسلام وان نجتمعوا بكم فى ابرك وقت سالمين // وفى اعلى الدرجات
راقين ءامين والسلام يخص الحضرة البهية على الدوام والسلام / حرر سنة / ١٣٢٦ /
رمضان المعظم / ٢٢ فيه // وان تيسرت جلود سبع ونمر تامة بمخابثها وما / فيها
شيء غائب منها الله يزيد فى وسعكم / وايضا نصيب زبد من الطيب نريدوه للدواء
/ وان هو متعسر فلا حرج المحل واحد الله يبارك / فيكم ءامين والسلام

المتغنى بالغنى
القدوسى محمد بن السيد
الشريف السنوسى
سنه ١٣٢٠

In the name of God, the Merciful, the Compassionate. The blessing and peace of God upon our lord Muḥammad, his family, and companions.

From the insignificant servant of his Master, Muḥammad `Ābid al-Sharīf.

To the exalted king and eminent sultan, our sultan, Sultan `Alī Dīnār. May God Most High allow him to continue to attain the crests of glory, and breathe the gentle breezes of laud and praise. Amen.

After the bestowal of greetings, we hope in God that your petitions will never stop coming to me. I inform you that I received what our subject and servant Shaykh `Abd al-Qādir al-Azraq brought with him for me from [your] majesty. I received from him 100 *Majīdī* dollars in cash and the ghee, honey, leather, and so forth. By God, I am unable to compensate you; everything that arrived exceeded our highest expectations and made us exceedingly happy. Everything came to us safely, may God be praised. According to the custom of the *'ulamā'*, when they fall short in compensating their friends, they take the mosques as their abode and make prayer their device.

Our children, your son Muḥammad al-Sharīf and his brethern, greet you, rejoicing at what has come to them from you. May God bless you, acknowledge your endeavor, and accept your achievement. Each thing is even better than the next, but we troubled you; forgive us. When we see our countries as one, and see the true affection that will not fail while life endures, if God wills, then we hope that God may bring that [sentiment] to completion through a meeting. Amen, amen, for He is able to do that.

Further, your greetings have reached us, and all your instructions of good guidance and advice. They are accepted, and placed upon the forehead,[4] for this is your custom and practice concerning us through the power of God.

We have sent out the brother Shaykh 'Abd al-Qādir al-Azraq to come to you. If God wills, you will meet with him while you are well. We have charged him urgently to remain with our camels in the vicinity of your country. If you indeed look upon him as we think you do, we do not have to instruct you in regard to him. He has some affairs we have instructed him to settle in your most beautiful land, and weapons to sell there. May he bring this to a good end. It was intended that Abū Bakr al-Ghadāmsī would come to you together with him, but he has not yet come [back]. God willing, he will come to you according to your command and report to you orally. If God wills, this will find you in power and a high position. Our order is that he should stay in the vicinity of your places to be an intermediary between us and you. He will deliver letters to you and return, and take care of the necessary affairs--or rather, it is you who will take care of them for us, for he is the one in need. So have him travel [back] to us quickly, and before him the son of all, Faraj, whom we pray to God may be near to us.

Inform us concerning what is necessary. May God reward you with goodness, for the country is yours, and may God unite us with you quickly. If

God wills, we will encourage the merchants and write to them to bring weapons to your beautiful land--may the Lord of Creation preserve it.

So advise us and inform us, and let us know about everything, as is your custom with us. May God preserve you for our sake. Moreover, I ask God to give you pardon, good health, power, perpetual sovereignty and the power of Islam. May we meet safe and sound in the most blessed of times, enjoying the highest positions. Amen. Greetings to [your] splendid majesty forever. Farewell. It was written in the year 1326, on the twenty-third of Ramaḍān *al-Mu`aẓẓam*[5] /19 October 1908.

And if it is possible [please send] complete skins of lions and leopards with their claws, with nothing missing from them. May God increase your capability. Also a portion of the best butter; which we want for medicine. But if it is difficult, then there is no problem, for [our] country is one. May God bless you. Amen. Farewell.

Illuminated with the Most Holy Light
Muḥammad b. al-Sayyid al-Sharīf al-Sanūsī[6]
Year 1320/1902-1903

1. Triaud, "Relations," pp. 1089-1093; armed retaliation against French advances began late in 1906.

2. Ibid., p. 1012, note 137.

3. Lacuna, conjectural reading.

4. Pressing a letter to one's forehead was a way of showing respect to its author. In 1912, the traveller Rosita Forbes saw bedouins respond to a letter from Sanūsī leader Muhammad Idrīs: "They read the superscription reverently and then one by one kissed it with passionate earnestness and gravely pressed it to their foreheads" (Forbes, *Kufara*, p. 8).

5. *Al-Mu`aẓẓam*: common epithet of the month of Ramāḍān.

6. Note that Muḥammad `Ābid uses the name Muḥammad al-Sharīf in his seal.

DOCUMENT 3

Communication was at best slow and unreliable in a world of vast distances, rugged terrain, and many accidental misfortunes. Sudanic rulers took a particularly dim view of those who delayed their couriers unnecessarily, while the deliberate infliction of such delays was one of the time-tested provocative pressure tactics of regional politics.[1] Document 3 was written in Kufra late in 1908 to accompany `Abd al-Qādir al-Azraq's caravan of November-December. Its primary purpose was to assure `Alī Dīnār that his messenger had been delayed in Kufra only for the honorable purpose of allowing him to celebrate the *`Īd al-Fiṭr* in comfortable surroundings.

بسم الله الرحمن الرحيم وصلى الله على سيدنا محمد وءاله وصحبه مع التسليم / الى
الحضرة الفخيمة والسلطنة العظيمة العلم الشهير الجليل الكبير ذى الهمة العالية والعزيمة
الماضية / والسطوة الكاملة والرافة الشاملة السلطان الكامل صاحب الحكم العادل ذى
القول الوافى ومحل / اللطف الكامل الشافى محبنا الاوحد سلطاننا السلطان على دينار
اعلى الله صيته فى جميع الاقطار بحرمة / نبيه المختار صلى الله عليه وسلم وشرف
وعظم وكرم امين وبعد اهداء تحيات تبارى نسمات الصبا بلطفها / وتزدري نشر
خمائل الربي بعرفها خاصا بكم سائلا عنكم ادام الله لنا بقاكم ويسر لنا رؤيتكم
ولقاءكم فقد ورد علينا / وشرفنا واسرنا ورود كتابكم المرصع بخطابكم فقبلناه ولتلاوته
مرارا قراناه فازداد السرور بسلامة تلك الذات الزكية / والاخلاق المرضية واسرنا كثيرا
كثيرا شدة اهتمامكم بحوائجنا مع اننا ما لنا قدرة على مكافاتكم الا كما قال الشاعر/
فلا شكرتك ما حيت وان امت فلتشكرتك اعظمى فى قبرها والحمد لله قد اتصلنا به

ونحن بخير صحبة الاخ خديمنا / وصديتنا الشيخ عبد التادر الازرق وصلنا بخير لله
الحمد وقد اعطيتموه الخير وعظمتموه وما فعلتم معه الا ما / يسرنا ويزيد فى عزه
وراحته كما هى دابكم معه ومع من اتاكم   خصوصا من طرفنا فالله سبحانه وتعالى
يديم علاكم و / و[2]   يضاعف عزكم وتوتكم على امدائكم حتى تكون جيوش الاعداء
من اصابة سهام سعادتكم حائرة والقوة والتاييد / والسلطنة حول مركز سيادتكم
دائرة ولا زالت العلياء ملقية اليك بالمقاليد والايام والليالى خادمة لكم / بعز عتيد وفتح
جديد ومجد اكيد ولم يحدث بطرفنا سوى الخير وانتم فيه نرجوا الله ان تكون
(الاجوبة)[3] / كلها السابقة منا اليكم اتصلت بيديكم وانتم بخير وعافية ثم ان
نخص الحضرة بالسلام ونستعطف / منها الخاطر الكريم على الدوام والسلام / حرر
سنة ١٣٢٦   فى رمضان المكرم   ٢٧ / بل فى شوال ٩ / مبارك شهر
الصيام ان شاء الله عائد علينا وعليكم سنينا / واعوام بجاهه افضل الصلاة والسلام
وصيامنا بالاحد / وقد تاخر الاخ الحامل الى ان عيد معنا عيد الفطر وعيدنا بيوم /
الثلاثاء ان شاء الله عيد سعيد يعيد عليكم بالعز والنصر

المتفىء بالفو

التدوسى محمد بن السيد

الشريف السنوسى

سنه ١٢٢٠

In the name of God, the Merciful, the Compassionate. The blessings and peace of God upon our lord Muḥammad, his family and companions.

To the eminent majesty and mighty sultan, the famous man of distinction, honorable and great, possessed of lofty aspiration and resolute intent, perfect authority and all-embracing compassion, the perfect sultan, master of just judgment, true of word, a source of perfect salutory kindness, our beloved and unique sultan, Sultan `Alī Dīnār. May God elevate his prestige in all quarters through the sanctity of His chosen prophet, may God bless him and grant him peace, honor, might and nobility. Amen.

After the bestowal of salutations that compete with the breezes of the east wind in their pleasantness and in their fragrance make little of the smell of aromatic bushes, especially for you, asking about you. May God prolong your life for our sake, and enable us to see you and to meet you. Your letter, inlaid with the gems of your words, has arrived, and gave us honor and joy. We kissed it, and we read it, reciting it aloud several times. Our joy increased at [learning of] the health of that pure self and examplary character. We rejoiced at your solicitude in regard to our needs, although we are unable to compensate you. However, as the poet has said: "If I have not thanked you while alive, then let my bones thank you from the grave." Praise be to God, we have received it [the letter], while we were well, from the brother, our servant and friend, Shaykh `Abd al-Qādir al-Azraq. He reached us safely, praise be to God. You treated him well and made much of him, and treated him only in ways that pleased us and increased his standing and comfort, as is your custom with him and with those who come to you, especially from our side. May God Most Exalted and High prolong your eminence and redouble your might and power over your enemies, so that enemy armies become baffled targets for your excellency's arrows. May power and support and royal authority encompass your lordship's seat of power. May high status always be proffered to you with its authority. May days and nights serve you with future might, new conquest and certain glory. Here nothing but good has occurred; may the same be true for you.

We beseech God that all the letters we sent to you before reached you while you were well and in good health. Thereupon we bestow a farewell upon [your] majesty, and ask for your kind friendship always. Farewell.

It was written in the year 1326 on Ramaḍān *al-Mukarram*[4] 27/23 October 1908. No; on Shawwāl 9/4 November 1908.

If God wills, may we celebrate [the completion of] a blessed month of fasting for years and years [to come], through the influence of him [the prophet], may blessings and peace be upon him. Our fast began on Sunday; the brother who is the bearer has delayed to celebrate the *'Īd al-Fiṭr* with us. We celebrated the *'Īd* on Tuesday. If God wills, you have celebrated a happy *'Īd* with power and victory.

Illuminated with the Most Holy Light
Muḥammad b. al-Sayyid al-Sharīf al-Sanūsī
Year 1320/1902-1903

1. Kapteijns and Spaulding, *After the Millennium*, p. 30.
2. Dittography.
3. Lacuna, conjectural reading.
4. *Al-Mukarram*: a common epithet of the month of Ramāḍān.

DOCUMENT 4

Document 4 is the first of several letters written in Kufra near the close of 1908 for dispatch to ʿAlī Dīnār early the following year with a caravan led by Muḥammad Yūnus. The primary purpose of Document 4 was to introduce the Sanūsī ambassador Abū Bakr al-Ghadāmsī, whose presence the Dār Fūr sultan had specifically requested. The ambassador had been summoned promptly, had arrived in Kufra, and would now join the caravan of Muḥammad Yūnus. A second concern of Document 4 was the reception in al-Fāshir of the party of Majābra merchants from Jalo who accompanied the ambassador. Private Islamic merchants from the Mediterranean world, accustomed to traveling about with comparatively few political constraints and to offering their wares through bargaining in a competitive market environment, often found the commercial usages of Sudanic monarchs strange and restrictive. The letter presented here, perhaps in response to previous misunderstandings, attempted to smooth the reception of the Sanūsī merchants in al-Fāshir by addressing in advance two common points of possible controversy. The Majābra, as importers of arms and luxury goods, would be dealing directly with the court of Dār Fūr and would probably not be allowed to offer their wares competitively on the open market; therefore the king was urged to reward them fairly. Since Sudanic kings often sought to coopt the services of reliable foreign merchants by inviting them to become royal agents,[1] and since the Sanūsī authorities wished neither to lose the services of Muḥammad Yūnus and his followers nor to see them placed in an embarrassing position by having to refuse a royal offer, the king was tactfully warned *not to try to divert them from their assigned mission.*

بسم الله الرحمن الرحيم / حضرة صفوة الاكارم الاماجد الجامع ما تفرق من مكارم

المحامد غرة جبين الشرف الاجل وقرة عين المجد الاعلى بدر العالمين / الذى اضاءت

به نواحيها ومنار المئاثر الذى اهتدى به ساريها الملك الجليل القدر والمقدار سلالة

السلاطين الاكرمين / مولانا السلطان على دينار اعلى الله مقامه وبلغه من خير الدارين
مرامه ولا زالت ثغور الامال بوجوده بواسم ورياح / الاقبال بسعوده نواسم ولا برحت
خلافته على رعاياه وارفة الظلال سابغة الانعام والافضال ءامين بعد اهداء / سلام يحفه
من التكريم ما يليق بذلك الجناب الكريم وثناء على محاسن تلك الشوائل تتمسك
بطيب شذاه نسمات / الشمائل فان الموجب لتسطيره والباعث الى رقمه وتحريره
السوال عن تلك المكارم التى هى لازهار الربا (كمائل) [2] / ابقاها الله تعلى تاجا لاعالى
المعالى وغياثا للرعايا والموالى وان جنح شريف الخاطر والبال العاطر الى السوال عن /
هذا الطرف فجميع من به يقتطف من رياض حسان الله ازهار الطرف مواظبون على
ما تعهده *الحضرة السرية من التوجه / التلبية والفواتح* السرية بدوام نصرة مولانا وبقائه
وتاييد رجال دولته واوليائه لا زالت هذه الدولة طراز (. . . .)[3] / الدول رافلة فى
العزة القعساء فى اضفى الحلل دعوت ربى واليه القبول ثم انه قد اتى سابقا من
الحضرة الامر بارسال / الشيخ ابا بكر الغدامسى الى الطرف السعيد ليكون ان
شاء الله على يديه لتلك النواحى الهداية والتاييد وكنا نترر / لرفيع الجناب بعدم
حضوره فى وقت وصول الجواب وواعدنا الحضرة بارساله عند قدومه وقد رجع بالسلامة
و (العافية)[2] / وها هو متوجه الى الرحاب الكرمية صحبة اخ الجميع محمد يونس
ومن معه من المجابره القاصدين المراحم الفخيمه فالله يغنمهم / السلامة والعافيه وعند
الاجتماع بهم يخبرونكم بالاحوال شفاها والمطلوب من المولى الكريم ان يجعل على يديه
نفع / العباد وان يصلح به الحاضر والباد ويوفق الجميع لاتباع سنه خير العباد وحتى
نكون جميعا من الفائزين فى يوم (الثناء)[2] الصالح/ ولا تحتاج المكارم الحاتميه الى
التوصية عليه وعلى من معه فيما لا بد منه من الاحوال الضروريه ولا زال الدعاء (منا)[2]
/ للحضرة مبذولا والله سبحانه وتعلى يتولاه اجابة وقبولا ويحفظ مجدكم ويديم

سعدكم وازكى السلام يشمل من لاذ بالمقام / ومن عندنا ضونا السيد محمد عابد والسيد محمد ادريس والسيد محمد الرضى وجميع الاخوة يخصون الحضرة باعطر التحية / والدعات الخيريه والسلام تاريخ سلخ قعده سنه ١٢٢٦

المقتبس النور
القدوسى احمد ابن
السيد الشريف
السنوسى
١٢٢١

In the name of God, the Merciful, the Compassionate.

[To] the presence of the best of the most honorable and illustrious, who unites what was dispersed in regard to noble characteristics and praiseworthy deeds, at the very forefront of the most distinct nobility, the epitome of most eminent glory, the full moon of the universe, through whom its regions are illuminated, a beacon of glorious deeds to guide him who travels through the night, the king elevated in power and majesty, descendant of the most noble sultans, our master, Sultan `Alī Dīnār. May God elevate his position and cause him to attain what he desires from the good things of both worlds. May hopes not cease to smile because of his presence, and the winds of prosperity do not cease to blow because of his good fortune. May his vicarship over his flock continue to extend protection and permit acts of kindness and merit. Amen.

After the bestowal of a greeting encompassed by tribute befitting that noble eminence, and reverence for the merits of this loftiness, to the aroma of whose fragrance clings the aura of his fine qualities, the purpose for writing it and the reason for its recording and composition is to inquire about these noble deeds, which are more perfect than the flowers of the aromatic bushes. May God Most High keep him as a crown for the highest nobles and a support for the subjects and clients. Should the noble and fragrant heart and mind be inclined to ask about these parts, here everyone is gathering flowers from the edge of the beautiful gardens of God, persevering in what the high ranking majesty has enjoined with regard to the inclination of the heart and the opening of the soul toward the eternal victory of our master and his preservation, and toward the support of the men of his state and his holy men. May this state continue to be the embroidered train . . . of nations, trailing in the most copious garments and firmly established power.[4] This I ask my Lord, with Whom is acceptance.

Previously I received [your] majesty's instructions to send Shaykh Abū Bakr al-Ghadāmsī to the south so that through his presence, God willing, there would be guidance and support for those parts. We reported to your sublime excellency that he was not present at the time of the receipt of the letter, but we promised your majesty to send him upon his arrival. Now he has returned safe and well, and has set out to [your] noble court together with the brother to all, Muḥammad Yūnus, and those of the Majābra accompanying him who seek magnanimous compassion. May God grant them security and good health. When you meet them they will inform you about the state of affairs orally. What is asked of the generous lord is to put into his hands what benefits the worshipers, to be of benefit to the settled folk and nomads, and to grant all success in following the *sunna* of the best of the worshipers, so that we may all be among the triumphant on the Day of Rightful Commendation. There is no need for [his] unerringly noble [majesty] to direct him and those with him, for they have no escape from pressing affairs. We will not cease to exert ourselves in prayer for [his] majesty. May God Most Glorious and High take charge of him in fulfillment and acceptance, and preserve your glory and prolong your happiness.

The purest of greetings comes to all who take refuge in your noble presence. Here our twin brother al-Sayyid Muḥammad `Ābid, al-Sayyid Muḥammad Idrīs and al-Sayyid Muḥammad al-Riḍā, and all the *ikhwān* bestow on [your] majesty the most fragrant of salutations and benificent prayers. Farewell. Date: End of [Dhu'l-] Qa`da 1326/24 December 1908.

He who has acquired the Most Holy Light

Aḥmad b. al-Sayyid al-Sharīf al-Sanūsī

1321/1903-1904

1. For example, see the career of Ṭāhir walad Aḥmad of Document 19.

2. Lacuna, conjectural translation.

3. Lacuna.

4. Conjectural translation.

DOCUMENT 5

Several members of the incumbent generation of Sanūsī leaders initiated and maintained cordial relations with `Alī Dīnār. Document 5, written in Kufra late in 1908 to accompany the southbound caravan of Muḥammad Yūnus early the next year, was a friendly letter from the junior Sanūsī dignitary `Alī al-Khaṭṭābī. The letter was personal in character and did not overtly raise issues of politics or commerce.

بسم الله الرحمن الرحيم / الى من استطى من ذرى المجد اعلاها واقتصى من وافر الطيبات اغلاها عمدة الاجلة / الازكياء الفظلا [1] ونخبة الاعزة الاذكياء النبلا حبنا الاصفى ومحبنا الاوفى ذى المكانة والاعتبار / مولانا السلطان على دينار اجد الله بعنايته سعادته وايد فى غايته سيادته ءامين / السلام الاسنى وتحياته المباركات الحسنى عليكم ورحمة الله وبركاته وتعمكم نفحاته وبعد فموجبه / السوال عنكم وعن كلية احوالكم اجرى الله صالحاتها طبق ءامالكم بمنه وكرمه وان تفضلتم عنا بالسوال / فان جميع اخوتنا وكافة الاخوان بحمد الله وتوفيقه على احسن حال ادام الله ذلك على الجميع بحرمة / النبى الشفيع صلى الله عليه وسلم ومجد وعظم ولم يحدث ما يتاكد رفعه سوى الخيرات وتزايد المسرات / ونقول انكم فى جميع ذلك ان شاء الله مدى الاوقات والساعات هذا وقد تقدم منا لحضرتكم كتاب / نقول ان شاء الله اتصل بكم وها هو اخونا محمد يونس قادم الى رحابكم السليمة المرعية صحبة السلامة / والعافية وصحبته منا لكم ما يصلكم بالهناء والعافية ان شاء الله على وجه البركة ولا تزالون متحوبين / بصالح الدعوات فى الخلوات والجلوات وعلى الله القبول انه اكرم مسؤل حفظكم الله ورعاكم وادام انسكم / وهناكم ودمتم فى شرف لا يزول

وترف برضوان الله موصول هادين مهدين دالين على الخير وبه عاملين مدى / الايام

والسنين واتم السلام واكمله يهدى منا الى حضرت انجالكم [2] المكرمين ويهم سائر

الاتباع والمجير ومن عندنا مسلم / عليكم كافة الاخوه والاخوان والمجير والسلام

تاريخ غرة حجة سنة ١٣٢٦ / عبد ربه على الخطابى / ابن السيد محمد الشريف /

الضياء بالضو القدوسى

على ابن السيد الشريف السنوسى

١٣٢٢

In the name of God, the Merciful, the Compassionate.

To him who mounts the highest pinnacles of glory and penetrates to the source of the most precious of abundant good things, pillar of the most eminent, purest, and outstanding ones, the epitome of the most powerful, intelligent and noble, our purest beloved and most faithful friend, possessed of standing and esteem, our master, Sultan `Alī Dīnār. May God, through His providence, renew his happiness and through His design support his rule . Amen. The most radiant greetings to you, and His best and blessed salutations, and God's mercy and blessings. May His fragrance envelop you.

Thereafter: The purpose [of this letter] is to ask about you and all your affairs. May God make them successful according to your hopes, by His grace and kindness. Should you do us the favor of asking about us, all our brothers and all the *ikhwān*, with praise to God and [through] His favor, are in the best of conditions. May God prolong that for all, out of respect for the interceding prophet, may God bless him and grant him peace, glory and greatness. Nothing worthy of report has happened but good things and an increase of what is pleasing. We hope that you will be in exactly that [situation], if God wills, through [all] the times and hours.

We sent a letter to your majesty before, and we hope that, God willing, it has arrived. Now our brother Muḥammad Yūnus is coming to your safe and protected regions, safe and sound and in good health, bringing from us to you what you may receive in wellbeing and good health, with God's will and through His blessing. May you always continue to refrain from sin, through devout prayers in private and in public. Acceptance is with God, for He is the Most Generous Fulfiller of Requests. May God preserve you, guard you, prolong your life, and give you good health. May you remain in an eminence that does not pass, and in luxury that, with God's favor, will be continuous, guiding and rightly-guided, leading to what is good and acting in accordance with it, throughout the days and years.

The most perfect and complete of farewells comes from us to the presence of your most noble offspring, and embraces all the followers and [their] protector. From our side all the brothers, the *ikhwān*, and [their] protector greet you. Farewell. Dated the first day of [Dhu'l-] Ḥijja in the year 1326/25 December 1908. The worshiper of his Lord, `Alī al-Khaṭṭābī b. al-Sayyid Muḥammad al-Sharīf.

Lit with the Most Holy Light

`Alī b. al-Sayyid al-Sharīf al-Sanūsī

1322/1904-1904

1. Spelled as shown.

2. Written above the line.

DOCUMENT 6

Document 6 was a friendly letter to `Alī Dīnār from the Sanūsī leader Muḥammad `Ābid. The letter was personal in character and did not overtly raise issues of politics or commerce. With the benefit of hindsight, however, one should note that Muḥammad `Ābid's relations with the Dār Fūr monarch were destined to prove more significant than were those of most of his kinsmen, for as the Sanūsī guardian assigned to Kufra during the turbulent years ahead he was to become the most important liason between the brotherhood and Dār Fūr.

ولو لا رجاءي بان سنلتقي وان يجمع الله ما بيننا / لسارعت الروح شوقا اليك
ولكنها قنعت بالمنا / نسأل الله الاجتماع / ءامين / بسم الله الرحمن الرحيم وصلى الله
على سيدنا محمد وءاله وصحبه مع التسليم / الى مقام حضرة سيد الموالى وبهجة الايام
والليالى نادرة الزمان وتنجية الاوان من اليه تنتهى الامال والي / حرمه حط[1] الرحال
معدن العرفان ومطلب الاحسان امير المومنين وسلطاننا سلطان المسلمين الذى خصه
الله / بالغلب والدين وقواه على اعداه والمشركين بقدرة سيد المرسلين صلى الله عليه
وسلم وشرف وعظم وكرم السلطان / المؤيد بالله نخص بذالك سلطاننا ومولانا السلطان
على دينار ايد الله معاقد العز بوجوده وايد معالى / المجد ببره وجوده ولا زالت روضة
عزه ناضرة واعين التوفيق بالسعادة له ناضرة ولا فتئ مؤيدا منصورا / مستبشرا
صدورا متصفا بالفضل الاتم والمجد الاشم ءامين كما قيل ءامين ءامين لا ارض
بواحدة حتى اضيف / اليها الف ءامين وبعد اهداء سلام تتبسم بالمحبة والمودة ثغور
سطوره وترتم بصدق الاخلاص احرف / منشوره وتسليمات تتعطر الاكوان بطيب
نشرها وتحيات تتلالا فى سماء الطروس بدورها ويلوح فى ءافاق / الاوراق زهورها

مختصة بكم مقيمة معكم لا تنفك عنكم ادام الله لنا بقاكم وسهل لنا رؤيتكم ولقاكم
ءامين ⸝ فموجبه شدة التشوف والتشوق لاجوبتكم واخباركم المحبوبة قربها الله منا فى
اسر وقت واعلامكم بان ولله ⸝ الحمد بعد الاجوبة المتقدمة اليكم نرجوا الله ان تكون
وصلتكم وقبلت يديكم وانتم بخير وما تجدد بعدها ⸝ سوى الخير وانتم فيه ان شاء
الله من غير شك وان اخينا محمد يونس وصل للطرف بخير واقام هنا اياما ⸝ لما
تاخر منه وتوى ابله وها هو ان شاء الله يصلكم سالما بخير وعافية هو ورفقاؤه ويفيدكم
شفاها بجميع ⸝ الاحوال والله يكن [2] فى العون هذا وانى لا زلت اترقب اخباركم
واجوبتكم وما يلزمكم بحوله وقوته على الراس ⸝ والعين وادعوا لكم ءاناء الليل واطراف
النهار وعلى الله القبول هذا وسلام ومزيد احترام يخصكم ⸝ مدى الليالى والايام بغاية
الادب والاحترام ودمتم فى اعز النعم والسلام عليكم سيدى ورحمة الله ⸝ وبركاته فى
كل لمحه ونفس عدد ما وسعه علم الله والسلام ⸝ تحريرا⸝ فى ⸝ حجه ٧ ⸝ سنه
١٣٢٦ ⸝ ولا مواخذة فى قلة الادب معكم

المتضىء بالضو
القدوسى محمد بن السيد
الشريف السنوسى
سنه ١٢٢٠

Had it not been for my hope that we would meet,
And that God would eliminate the distance between us,
Then my spirit would have hastened in longing for you,
But it contented itself with this hope.
We ask God to unite us.
Amen

In the name of God, the Merciful, the Compassionate. The blessings and peace of God upon our lord Muḥammad, his family and companions.

To the residence of [his] majesty, the lord of lords, the splendor of days and nights, unique in [his] time, the salvation of the age, with whom hopes reach their destination, and at whose sanctuary nomads dismount, the mine of knowledge, who commands good deeds, commander of the faithful, our sultan, the sultan of the Muslims, whom God has distinguished with victory and in religion, and whom God gave power over his enemies and the polytheists, through the might of the lord of the messengers, may God bless him and grant him peace, and may [He] give eminence, greatness and nobility to the sultan, who is supported by God, namely, our sultan and lord Sultan `Alī Dīnār. May God support the axes of power through his presence, and sustain through his existence the peaks of glory. May the garden of his power never cease to bloom, and may the eyes of good fortune continue to look with favor upon him. May he not cease to be divinely-aided and victorious, happy, with an untroubled heart, in the most complete favor and most honorable glory. Amen. As it is said: "Amen, amen. I cannot be content with one, unless a thousand 'amens' are added to it."

After the bestowal of a greeting, the lips of whose lines smile with love and affection, written with the candor of sincerity, printed letters and greetings that perfume the cosmos through the aroma they emit, and salutations whose full moons beam in the heaven of paper sheets, and whose flowers are radiant on the horizons of leaves of paper, especially for you, for always, inseparable from you. May God preserve you for us, and make it easy for us to see you and meet you. Amen. Its purpose is to express strong anticipation and longing for your beloved letters and news. May God bring them to us in the happiest of times. Also, to let you know that, praise be to God, after the recent letters to you, I am hoping in God that these reached you and came into your hands, while you were well. May nothing new have come about thereafter except what is good, and is good for you, if God wills, without any doubt. Our brother Muḥammad Yūnus came to us safely. He stayed here for a few days, delaying to strengthen his camels. Lord willing he will come to you safe and sound and in good health, he and his companions, and inform you orally about everything. May God give support. I have never stopped waiting for your news and letters, and through His might and power, it is my pleasure [to provide] what you require. I pray for you night and day, and acceptance is with God. A greeting and abundant respect come to you by night and by day, with the highest of refinement and respect. May you remain in the most glorious comfort. Peace be upon you, my lord, and God's mercy and blessings, at every glance and breath, as many as God's wisdom accommodates. Farewell. Written on 7 [Dhu'l-] Ḥijja in the year 1326/31 December 1908. Pardon my lack of manners with regard to you.

Illuminated with the Most Holy Light
Muḥammad b. al-Sayyid al-Sharīf al-Sanūsī
Year 1320/1902-1903

[1]Reading Ḥ Ṭ Ṭ for N Ḥ Ṭ.

[2]Spelled as shown.

DOCUMENT 7

Document 7, a final letter prepared for dispatch from Kufra to Dār Fūr with the caravan of Muḥammad Yūnus early in 1909, addressed some of `Alī Dīnār's practical concerns. The Sanūsī leader sent `Alī Dīnār a horse, a gift eminently appropriate to a king. The impending arrival of the ambassador Abū Bakr al-Ghadāmsī was confirmed. The letter also conveyed a muted implicit critique of the course of the recently established commercial relations between Dār Fūr and the Sanūsiyya. From Muḥammad `Ābid's perspective northern merchants in Dār Fūr had been obliged to wait longer than had been anticipated for consignments of slaves, and the return to Kufra of their caravan had been delayed. The king was urged to expedite the completion of their affairs.

الحمد لله وحده الحاق خير يخص الحضرة العلية بدوام / العز والخير فبينما نحن

نجهزوا الجواب الذى مع محمد يونس وفى تمام كتابته قدم / اخونا سيدي ابا[1] بكر

الغدامسى من المحل الذي كان فيه يتقضى مصلحة ويرجع نحين / وصل بادرنا فى

تجهيزه اليكم حسبما امرتم وواعدناكم بقدومه عليكم فها هو ان / شاء الله يصلكم مع

الاخ محمد يونس ومن معه بخير وعافية وانى رهين اشارتكم / فى التى تلزم عرفونا

محلكم والاخ الاعز غيث وابنى فرج نرجوا الله انهم قريب / منا ما نوصوكم عليهم

ولا نامروكم بقدومهم عاجلا طول الله عمركم وقواكم على / عدوكم وبلغكم مناكم

وجمعنا بكم على خير ولا قدرة لى على مكافاتكم الا الدعاء / الذى بحول الله لا نفتر

عنه ومبارك عليكم هذا الحصان اركبكم الله سرج القدرة فى / الدنيا والاخرة ان

شاء الله يصلكم مع صاحبه بخير سالما محفوظا ودمتم ودام لنا / بقاكم ءامين

والسلام عليكم ورحمة الله عدد كلمات الله فى كل لمحة ونفس / عدد ما وسعه علم

الله ءامين سيدى / حرر / ٧ حجة / فى / سنه / ١٢٢٦ / وبكم منتظرين العبيد الذين عرفتكم عليهم فى الاجوبة السابقة لان الحاجة / بهم اكيدة مع قدوم خديمكم فرج وغيث عاجلا عاجلا حرسكم الله / بعينه التى لا تنام ءامين

المتضىء بالضو

القدوسى محمد بن السيد

الشريف السنوسى

سنه ١٢٢٠

Praise be to God alone. A beneficent enclosure comes to [your] sublime majesty, with everlasting power and goodness.

While we were preparing the letter which is with Muḥammad Yūnus, and when it had been completely written, our brother Sīdī Abū Bakr al-Ghadāmsī arrived from the place where he had been to take care of business and to return. When he arrived, we promptly equipped him [for the journey] to you, according to your order and our promise that he should come to you. If God wills he will come to you with the brother Muḥammad Yūnus and those with him, safely and in good health. I am depending on your instructions in regard to what is needed. Let us know your situation. We pray to God that the most distinguished brother Ghayth and my son Faraj are [now] close to us, and that we do not [need to] advise you with regard to them nor bid you send them quickly.

May God lengthen your life, give you power over your enemy, bring you to your appointed destiny, and unite us with you in goodness. I am not able to reward you except with prayers in which, through God's power, I will not falter.

May this horse be blessed for you. May God make you to ride in the saddle of power in this world and the next. If God wills, it will come to you with its keeper, safe and sound and in a good state. May your life last, and may you continue to live for our sake. Amen. Peace be upon you, and God's mercies, as numerous as the Words of God, in every glance and breath, as many as God's wisdom accommodates. Amen, my lord.

It was written on 7 [Dhu'l-] Ḥijja in the year 1326/31 December 1908.

With you are people awaiting slaves, about whom I informed you in the previous letters, for the matter needs urgent attention very, very quickly with the arrival of your servant Faraj and Ghayth. May God protect you with His eye that does not sleep. Amen.

Illuminated with the Most Holy Light
Muḥammad b. al-Sayyid al-Sharīf al-Sanūsī
Year 1320/1902-1903

[1]Spelled as shown.

DOCUMENT 8

Document 8 is Muḥammad `Ābid's postscript or addendum to another letter now lost; it is not dated, but may be placed in the last half of 1909 or the first quarter of 1910 on the basis of internal evidence. Muḥammad `Ābid thanked `Alī Dīnār for the gift of a gun and a new seal, whose large octagonal impression first appears on this document; he also made discreet suggestions concerning the suitability of guns as presents for the Sanūsī children. In a more substantive vein Muḥammad `Ābid introduced to the sultan a caravan leader named Aḥmad Bū Kāda, apparently not previously known to the king; such endorsement for the probity of merchants in the southern trade was one of the important powers exercised by the Sanūsī leaders.[1] Muḥammad `Ābid lamented the difficulty of the times--a prolonged drought had set in--and he thanked `Alī Dīnār for supplying Kufra with provisions that the French-beleaguered *zāwiyas* of Chad were not in a position to provide.[2] The caravan leader Faraj had been unable to switch his camels in Kufra as was customary, and had been obliged to march on north after a month of rest in the oasis. Finally, in a fashion rather bold for the customary style of diplomatic exchange, the Sanūsī leader congratulated `Alī Dīnār on his defeat of the holdout Mahdist commander Sinīn Ḥusayn; he also thanked him for his kindness to the defeated Wadaian sultan Dūd Murra.

الحمد لله وحده وبه ثقتى الحاق خير ثم انى بايد المسرات والفرح المضاعف /
تناولت بندقتنا منكم مع جبخانتها وقبلناها وهي التى فى يدنا وما راينا اعظم منها
فلا اقدر اوصف لكم فرحتى وسروري / بكم وبها ثم الختم الذي والله كانكم
كاشفتم على قلبى وانى اريده منكم خصوصا اتمناه فالله سبحانه وتعالى يمد لنا فى /
عمركم ويزيد فى هممكم وكمالكم الذي خصصتم به دون خلق الله كما تروه فى

الجواب وانتم بخير ان شاء الله ثم ان ابنكم / فرج مكث ايام راحته وراحة جماله قدر ٢٥ يوما ووجهناه بها لجهة البحر وعجلناه وفى ايام تاريخه نظنوه / بحول الله ما يتاخر حتى وان كان حصل له تعب وهو متوجه وضاعت له عن جمال وان شاء الله فداء عنكم / وحين ياتى نعرفوكم تفصيلا بحول الله وانتم بخير واسترحم الحضرة ان لا تؤاخذنا فى قلة ادبنا معها فى / مكاتيبنا وغيرها كما هو دابها حرسها الله وايدها ثم ان حامل هذا اليكم احمد بوكادة المجبري وفرحنا / به كثيرا حيث من مدة ما اتانا احد قاصد جهتكم ولا غيرها لان عامنا هذا تعبنا فيه كثيرا لقلة مؤنة الناس / فيه حتى فى البحر يشتكون منه كثيرا والله لا يعيده الا باحسن منه ولو لا ما اتانى من كرمكم وبركم العظيم مع ابنكم فرج / ما ادري ما يحصل فينا ابقاكم الله ملجأ للعباد ومنجا للزوار والوراد ثم ان الاخ غيث سمعناه قريب منا ونحن فى انتظاره / غاية وعندنا بعض لوازم سيدى مع الشيخ عبد القادر ونسترحم من الحضرة كما هى عادتها تاتنا سريعا سيدى / ودمتم لنا بخير وانى رهين اشاراتكم فيما تامروا او تعرفوا عنه دائما وسالتم عن عيالكم تريدون لهم بنادق سلاح / نفيدوكم عن عمرهم فعندكم ولد السنه هذه صام فيها وفقه الله لما يرضيه ويرضيكم وهو اسمه ولدكم محمد الشريف / واخوته صغار ادام الله عمركم لهم ءامين // وما حصل لنا من السرور يوم وورود درركم الحسان / ان سنين ومن معه ظفرتم بهم ووالله لا توصف / تلك المسرات زادكم الله قوة على المردة / ءامين سيدى / وما حصل بواداي ونزل بها فلا حول ولا قوة الا بالله / نرجوا الله ان ينصر الله بكم الاسلام حتى تمحى الكفرة / من تلك الديار وسمعنا انكم ارسلتم رسلا الى محمد صالح / وفعلتم معه فعل الكمل اسرنا ذالك والله غاية / كيف لا وانتم محل راحة عباد الله ومنجاهم ءامين /

المتفيء بالضو

القدوسي محمد

ابن السيد الشريف

السنوسي

سنه ١٢٦٠

Praise be to God Alone. In Him I trust. A blessed addendum.[3] Thereafter: I am overpowered by pleasure and redoubled joy. We have obtained our gun from you with its ammunition. We have received it, and it is in our hands. We have never seen a more splendid one. I cannot describe to you my joy and pleasure with you and with it. Then the seal--by God, it is as if you had looked into my heart and [saw] that I wanted and desired it in particular from you. May God Most Blessed and High extend your life and for our sake increase your zeal and the perfection which has been apportioned to you above all others of God's creation. You will see it [the seal] in the letter, [which will reach you], God willing, while you are well.

Your son Faraj stayed to rest himself and his camels for twenty-five days. Then we sent him off in the direction of the sea, and bade him hasten. At this moment we think that, by God's power, he will not be long even if he suffered hardship while on the road or lost camels. When he comes we will inform you of the details, while you, by God's power, are well.

I ask [his] majesty to kindly pardon us for our lack of protocol with him, in our letters and elsewhere, as is his custom. May God guard and aid him.

The one who is carrying this to you is Aḥmad Bū Kāda al-Majabrī. We are very happy with him, for for a long time no one has come to us heading toward your area, nor anywhere else, for during this year we have suffered much hardship due to the shortage of provisions for people. Even at the coast people have complained much about this. May God give us a new year that is better! Had it not been for what has come to me through your generosity and great kindness, via your son Faraj, I do not know what would have happened to us. May God preserve you as a refuge for the worshipers and a haven for pilgrims and travelers.

We heard that Brother Ghayth was near to us, and we are awaiting him with great anticipation.

My lord, we have [placed] a few requests for goods with Shaykh `Abd al-Qādir. We ask [your majesty} kindly that they, my lord, may come to us quickly, as is [your] custom. May you stay well, for our sake. I am forever subject to your instructions concerning what you order or what you inform us.

You ask about your children,[4] wanting [to send] guns as weapons for them. We are informing you of their ages. You have a son called Muḥammad al-Sharīf who has fasted [for the first time] this year; may God give him success in what pleases Him and you. His brothers are young. May God lengthen your life for their sake. Amen.

What joy we felt on the day your splendid achievements reached [our ears], that you triumphed over Sinīn and those with him. By God, this joy cannot be described. May God increase [your] power over the rebels. Amen, my lord.

As for what happened in Wadai and what befell it, there is no power and strength save with God. We hope, by God, that God will give Islam victory through you until the unbelievers have been obliterated from these lands. We heard that you dispatched messengers to Muḥammad Ṣāliḥ and dealt with him perfectly correctly. By God, that pleased us very much. How would it not, since you are a place of relief for the worshippers of God, and their refuge. Amen.

Illuminated with the Most Holy Light
Muḥammad b. al-Sayyid al-Sharīf al-Sanūsī
Year 1320/1902-1903

1. Triaud, "Relations," p. 846.

2. Ibid., pp. 1038-1039, 1074.

3. The letter to which this document is an addendum is not part of our collection and has probably been lost.

4. The author refers to his own children as children of `Alī Dīnār.

DOCUMENT 9

Document 9 is a business letter written in Kufra on 1 November 1909 in which the veteran Sanūsī leader Aḥmad al-Rīfī reported to `Alī Dīnār that a shipment of Dār Fūr ivory had arrived, and had been successfully exchanged for a number of guns ("goods") and ammunition ("their supplies"). Some of the weapons and munitions purchased were retained by the Sanūsī leaders, who expected to take a commission of about eight per cent on the Sudanese goods they brought to the Mediterranean coast, while the balance, after a delay, had been sent south to al-Fāshir.[1]

بسم الله الرحمن الرحيم / حضرة الجناب الارفع الاعز الامنع غرة جبين الفخر الاجلى
وقرة عين المجد الاعلى بحر الفضل الزاخر وبدر سماء / المحاسن والمفاخر مولانا
السلطان على دينار ابن السلطان زكريا ابن السلطان فضل العباسى ثبت / الله تواعد
مجده وجدد اوقات سعده ءامين بعد التحيات الزاهره والتسليمات الباهره فالموجب
لتسطيره / والباعث على ابرازه وتحريره السوال عن الخاطر الكريم والدعاء لحضرة
جنابكم بدوام العز والتكريم وان سالتم عن / احوال هذا الطرف فان سادتنا اولياء
النعمة رضى الله عنهم وجميع من معهم من الاخوان فى خير وعافية / ودوام الفضل
والامتنان ادام الله علينا وعليكم سوابغ نعمه وامطرنا جميعا بهوامع جوده وكرمه هذا /
وقد وصلنا من على جنابكم بعض السن سابقا ثم صدر امركم المطاع بصرف ثمنه فى
اللوازم المطلوبة للسياده / فاسرعنا فى امتثال ذلك الامر اداء لواجب حتكم واغتناما
لعظيم الاجر فحصل المطلوب وتم ذلك المرغوب / غير اننا رجعنا الزيادة من مؤنة
البضاعه لكونها محتاجا اليها وليس عنها غنى فى كل ساعه لنفادها / عند حصول

الشغل بها وليس لها باعه فتحصل من البضاعة سبعة وسبعون ومن مؤنتها خمسة ⸍
ءالاف وسبعمائة وسبعه ومحب الجميع الاخ الابر الحاج عبد الله البشار جهز لها ابلا
من نفسه وطلبها ⸍ يرسلها للسياده وسابقا كنا اكرينا عليها ولم يتم ذلك الكراء
فاستلم منا العدد المذكور وارسل من طرفه ⸍ صحبة ابله التى حملت ما ذكر الاخ
سعيد بن يعقوب الزويى فليكن من السيادة ببال وربنا سبحانه ييسر ⸍ الاحوال بحرمة
نبيه صلى الله عليه وسلم والصحب والال ابقاكم الله فى عز لا يزول ونعيم برضى
الله موصول ⸍ وافضل السلام وازكى التحية والاكرام يخصكم ويعم اللائذين بالمقام
ومن عندنا الساده وجميع الاخوان ⸍ يهدون لحضرتكم افضل السلام وحرر فى ١٧
شوال ⸍ سنه ⸍ ١٣٢٧ ⸍ احمد الريفى

In the name of God, the Merciful, the Compassionate.

[To] the presence of [his] most high, powerful, and invincible honor, the finest brow of most splendid glory, the delight of most eminent majesty, an overflowing ocean of kindness, a moon in the heaven of good qualities and glorious traits, our master Sultan `Alī Dīnār, son of Sultan Zakariyā, son of Sultan Faḍl al-`Abbāsī. May God make fast the foundations of his glory and extend for him the times of his good fortune. Amen.

After radiant salutations and dazzling greetings, the purpose for its recording and the motive for its composition and writing is to inquire about your noble person and to pray that the power and honor of your majesty be preserved. Should you ask about the conditions of these parts, our *sayyids*, the holy men of grace, may God be pleased with them, and all the *ikhwān* who are with them, are well and in good health, in continual grace and gratitude. May God prolong for us and for you His abundant favor, and rain down upon all of us streams of His generosity and liberality.

Previously some ivory came to us from your honor. Then your authoritative order was issued that its value should be disbursed for the necessities required by [your] lordship. We made haste to comply with that order, satisfying your interest and winning a great reward. The request was fulfilled, and what was desired was completed. However, we brought back the balance, for we need it and at no time can dispense with its presence. Seventy-seven of the goods and 5707 of their supplies were obtained.[2] Al-Ḥājj `Abd Allāh al-Bishār, the beloved of all, the most dutiful brother, has prepared camels of his own for them and asked to convey them to [your] lordship. Earlier we hired [camels] for them, but that hire was not completed. He received the said number from us and sent [them] from his side with his camels which carried what was mentioned by the brother Sa`īd b. Ya`qūb of the Zuwayya. [Your] lordship should take note. May our Lord, praise be to Him, facilitate the affairs out of respect for His prophet, may God bless him and grant him peace, and the companions and the family. May God maintain you in power that does not pass, and in comfort that is, with God's approval, continuous. The best of greetings and purest of salutations and respects come to you, and embrace those who seek refuge at the shrine.

Here the *sayyids* and all the *ikhwān* bestow upon your majesty the best of greetings. It was written on 17 Shawwāl in the year 1327/1 November 1909. Aḥmad al-Rīfī.

1. Triaud, "Relations," p. 936.
2. The author is referring to guns ("goods") and ammunition ("supplies").

DOCUMENT 10

Document 10 of 15 August 1910 exposes several dimensions of the maturing relationship between `Alī Dīnār and the Sanūsiyya. In it the leader of the brotherhood, Aḥmad al-Sharīf, appealed to the Dār Fūr sultan for the services of a scribe skilled in the Arabic script of the eastern Islamic world. He noted with appreciation the sultan's favorable reception of the Sanūsī diplomat Ibrāhīm al-Gharbī, though the letter did not touch upon the substance of his mission--the coordination of resistance on the part of `Alī Dīnār and Dūd Murra against the advance of the French. The letter also reported on the status of another of the king's shipments of ivory entrusted to Sanūsī hands, and asked that a quantity of coinage previously transported to Dār Fūr be sent back expeditiously.

بسم الله الرحمن الرحيم / الى حضرة صفوة الاكارم الاماجد الجامع ما تفرق من مكارم
المحامد غرة جبين الشرف الاجلى وقرة عين المجد الاعلى ذى / البطش الشديد والقوة
على اعدايه المسرى جلايل النعم لاودايه واحبايه [1] تاج العز والفخار حضرة مولانا
السلطان على / دينار ابن السلطان زكريا العباسى ادام الله عزه واقتداره وضاعف
مجده واعز انصاره ءامين بعد / اهداء اكرم السلام واسداء تحيات عظام تبارى
نسمات الصبا على خمايل الربا فقد وصلنا مكاتيبكم / الفخيمه المبدية ما عليه سيادتكم
من المودة السليمه فتلقيناها بالتبجيل والتعظيم واستفدنا من / سلامة الجناب الكريم
فحمدنا الله على ذلك وشكرناه على ما هنالك وان تفضلت السيادة عنا بالسؤال او
تحرى الخاطر / الشريف لشرح الحال فنحن وكافة الاخوان بخير وعافيه ونعم
متواليه ضافيه المامول من عظيم الجود و (الانعام) [2] / ان يشملنا واياكم بمواهبه

الدايمة الانسجام بحرمة النبى عليه افضل الصلاة والسلام وعامة احوال الطرف لله الحمد / ساره قاره لم يتجرد ما يجب اعلامكم به الا ازدياد الخيرات وتتابع المسرات ولا زلنا ان شاء الله مواظبين على / الدعوات الخيريه مبتهلين الى الله بكرة وعشيه ان يديم علوكم ويقهر عدوكم ويتولى برعايته حمايتكم ويتم من كل (قصد)[2] / رغبتكم انه ولى الاجابه واليه الرجوع والانابه ويكون فى شريف علم السياده ان بشير اوصل الى هذا الطرف على / احسن حال والهدية المصحوبة معه تويلت[1] منا بالقبول والاقبال وقد ذكرتم فى جوابكم المورخ ٢٤ ربيع الثانى / ما لحق حضرتكم السنية من السرور والابتهاج من جوابنا الوارد عليكم صحبة سيدى ابراهيم الغربى فحمدنا الله عز وجل / حيث الهمنا ثناءكم بما اودع فيكم من الفضايل الحميده والمكارم العديده والعدل والانصاف ادام الله عزكم / ونصركم ورفع بين الانام قدركم ونشر فى الخافقين ذكركم وفى الليلة التى قدم علينا فيها بشير ارسلنا السن / التى وصلتنا من على جنابكم الى بنغازى وامرنا المرسول بقضاء حاجتكم والاتياه بها عاجلا وها هو قادم على / حضرة سيادتكم الغلام بشير وامرناه بالرجوع على الاثر لاجل الاتياه ببتيه الدراهم التى عند الحضرة السلطانيه / والماسول من تعطفاتكم ان لا تتركوه يتعطل هناك بل بمجرد وصوله بحضرتكم سفروه ببتية الامانه لان اهلها / فى غاية الاحتياج اليها والله تعلى يديم وجودكم رحمة للعباد ويبسط عدلكم وفضلكم فى جميع البلاد انه ولى ذلك والمرجو / لما هنالك وبلغوا منا اتم السلام كافة من يلوذ لعلى جنابكم ومن عندنا يبلغكم جزيل السلام كافة الاخوة / والاخوان والمحبين ودمتم بخير وعافيه وسلام السلام يشملكم فى البدء والختام والسلام فى ٨ شعبان سنة / ١٣٢٨ // ومن جملة / المواصله / المطلوبه / من حضرة / جنابكم / ان كان / يوجد / كاتب خط / جيد جدا / يكتب الخط / المشرقى الناخر / رسلوه / لنا // ولا زال

السرور / يزداد بنا بتتابع اجوبتكم / المعلنه بالسرور والهناء ودوام (. . . .)[3] /
والمحبه الرابطه بيننا خصوصا فى / التعاقد على اعلاء كلمه الله و (. . . .)[3] / الله
جعلكم الله نورا للاسلام و (. . . .)[3] / وظلا للانام كما قال عليه (الصلاة . . .)[3]
/ السلطان ظل الله فى ارضه هذا (. . . .)[3] / يشمل كافه الانجال الفخام (. .)[3]
/ المولى على الدوام وعلى (انفسكم) / من عند الله مباركه طيبه

للقتبس النور
التدوسى احمد ابن
السيد الشريف
السنوسى
١٣٢١

In the name of God, the Merciful, the Compassionate.

To the presence of the epitome of the most honorable and glorious, who gathers what was scattered of noble deeds and praiseworthy acts, the finest brow of most splendid honor, the delight of most eminent glory, who possesses mighty force, and power over his enemies, the source of splendid favors for his friends and beloved ones, the crown of might and honor, [his] majesty, our master Sultan `Alī Dīnār, son of Sultan Zakariyā al-`Abbāsī. May God prolong his power and strength, redouble his glory, and make mighty his supporters. Amen.

After the bestowal of the most kindly greetings and the most sublime salutations, competing with the breezes of the east wind in the fragrant bushes, your splendid letters have reached us, revealing your lordship's perfect friendship. We have received them in deference and in exaltation. We have learned of the well-being of [your] noble excellency, and we praise God for that, and we thank Him for everything there.

Should [your] lordship favor us with an inquiry about us, or should the noble presence seek an elucidation of the state of affairs, we and all the *ikhwān* are well and in good health and in uninterrupted and abundant happiness.

What is hoped for from the One who is great in generosity and kindness is that He will surround us and you with His enduring gifts of harmony, out of respect for the prophet, upon whom be the best of prayers and peace. Praise be to God, all the affairs of the area proceed normally; nothing stands out that you should know about except for the increase in blessings and the succession of delights. If God wills, we shall not cease to persist in charitable prayers, supplicating God morning and evening to prolong your eminence, vanquish your enemies, take charge of protecting you through His care and satisfy your wishes in every way, for He grants requests, and to Him belong the return and the authorization.

Be it known to [your] noble lordship that Bashīr has arrived in these parts in the best condition. The present accompanying him we have received with appreciation and approval. You had already mentioned in your letter dated 24 Rabī` II [1328]/5 May 1910 [how much] pleasure and delight your lawful majesty found in our letter, which came to you with Sīdī Ibrāhīm al-Gharbī. We praised the Mighty and Exalted God that He has inspired us to express appreciation for the commendable virtues, numerous noble deeds, justice and equity, which He apportioned to you. May God prolong your power and victory, elevate your power among the people, and spread your reputation east and west. On the night in which Bashīr came to us we sent the ivory we received from your excellency to Benghazi. We ordered the messenger to dispose of your things and to return with [his purchases] quickly. The servant Bashīr is now coming to your lordship. We have ordered him to return at once to bring the rest of the *dirhams* which are with your sultanic majesty. What is hoped for out of your compassion is that you will not allow him to be delayed, but on the contrary, as soon as he has arrived in your presence, will send him on with the rest of the consignment, for its owners are in desperate need of it. May God Most High prolong your presence as a mercy to the worshipers, and extend your justice and kindness throughout the lands, for verily He can do that, and with Him lies all hope.

Convey our most perfect greetings to all who seek refuge with your eminent excellency. Here all the brethern, the *ikhwān* and the friends, send you abundant greetings. May you remain well, in good health, and at peace; may peace surround you from beginning to end. Farewell. On 8 Sha`bān in the year 1328/15 August 1910.

Among all the transactions requested from your excellency is--if he can be found--a scribe with very good handwriting who can write first-rate eastern script;[4] send him to us.

Our happiness never ceases to grow with the succession of your letters, manifesting joy and delight and the perseverance of and the bond of affection between us, especially in regard to the agreement about advancing the Word of God and . . God. May God make you a beacon for Islam . . . and a shade for mankind. As [Muḥammad], upon whom be [blessings and peace] said: "The sultan is the shadow of God upon His earth." This . . . embraces all the illustrious progeny . . the master forever, and from God and upon [yourselves], blessing and good.

He who has acquired the Most Holy Light
Aḥmad b. al-Sayyid al-Sharīf al-Sanūsī
1321/1903-1904

1. Spelled as shown.

2. Lacuna, conjectural reading.

3. The left margin of this second marginal text is not visible in our copy of the manuscript.

4. Eastern script differs from North African or *maghribī* script (M. Th. Houtsma et al., eds., *The Encyclopaedia of Islam* (Leiden: Brill, 1934), I, pp. 389-390). Unless otherwise indicated, the documents in this collection are written in *maghribī* script.

DOCUMENT 11

Despite longstanding disagreements `Alī Dīnār and Dūd Murra cooperated in resisting the French after the fall of Abesher; the Sanūsī emissary Ibrāhīm al-Gharbī came to al-Fāshir to help coordinate their efforts. Yet the alliance between the two rival kings could not be comfortable, and from `Alī Dīnār's point of view a particular source of irritation was the persistent, widespread unauthorized raiding carried out by members of the Sanūsī nomadic command of al-Dōr based on the Ennedi. Document 11 is an expulsion order of `Alī Dīnār, possibly written in about March 1910 during the Dār Fūr sultan's brief intervention in Dār Tāma, in which the king directed his wrath against Ṣāliḥ Abū Karīm, the Sanūsī commander of al-Dōr. In the event the Sanūsī leaders were able to smooth relations between the two men so that no dramatic rupture took place in that year. Following the defeat of Dūd Murra's forces by the French, Ṣāliḥ Abū Karīm was temporarily relieved of his command and summoned to Kufra for consultations.[1] It seems possible that he took Document 11 with him as evidence of the difficulties under which he labored, and that the Sanūsī leaders returned the document to `Alī Dīnār along with one of the later letters, possibly Document 12, through which they attempted to normalize relations between Dār Fūr and al-Dōr. Ṣāliḥ Abū Karīm returned to his command, and for a time his relations with Dār Fūr improved.

بسم الله[2] الرحمن الرحيم الحمد لله الوالي الكريم والصلاة علي سيدنا محمد وءاله مع

التسليم / وبعد فمن العبد الضعيف الحتير الذليل المعترف بذنبه والتقصير الراجي

عفو ربه التدير سلطان سلاطين / العالم وناشر لوا العدل بين من حارب وسالم امير

المؤمنين وسلطان المسلمين القايم في / مرضات رب العالمين المعتصم بالله الواحد المعين

السلطان علي دينار المنصور بالله تعالي ابن / المرحوم السلطان زكريا بن المرحوم السلطان

محمد الفضل الي صالح ابو كريم هداه مولاه امين بعد السلام ⁄ عليكم ورحمت الله تعالي وبركاته لديكم نعلمكم ان جوابكم وصل بطرفنا وفهمنا جميع ما ذكرتوه فيه ⁄ واعلموا ان الاعمور الحادثه منكم من الفساد والمغايره وعدم وقوفكم علي منهاج اولاد السنوسي ⁄ هذا لا يحتاج حتي وان الناس يخبروني به فاءنتم خالفتم الله والرسول وخالفتم ⁄ اولاد السنوسي في سيركم وافعالكم واني لا نرضاكم ما دمتم بهذه الصفه ولا نرضي اقامتكم ⁄ في حدودنا ولا خير في جواركم فالحاصل بوصول امرنا هذا اليكم قوموا من بلادي وابعدوا ⁄ في بلدا غيره تعيشكم لاءني لا نرضي الفتن والشواشر واما ما ذكرتوه من كلام الناس بحيث ⁄ انهم يسبوكم عندنا ابن من تكون انت من الناس حتي واني بابالي ونصغ [3] لكلام الناس ⁄ في حقكم فقد انذرتك ولا ظلمتك انكان توجهت من بلادنا خير لك وان لم تقم وتتوجه ⁄ فقد ظلمت نفسك و السلام ⁄ سنه

١٢٢٨

In the name of God, the Merciful, the Compassionate. Praise be to God, the Noble Ruler. Blessings and peace upon our lord Muḥammad and his family.

Thereafter: From the humble, base and lowly servant, conscious of his sin and shortcoming, and hoping for the forgiveness of his powerful lord, the sultan of the sultans of the world, who spreads the banner of justice between the one at war and the one at peace, commander of the faithful and sultan of the Muslims, steadfast in the favor of the Lord of the Universe, who adheres to the One God, the Helper, Sultan `Alī Dīnār, the victorious with God Most High, son of the late Sultan Zakariyā, son of the late Sultan Muḥammad al-Faḍl.

To Ṣāliḥ Abū Karīm, may his Master guide him. Amen.

After greetings to you, and the mercy of God Most High and His blessings upon you, we inform you that your letter has reached us. We have understood all that you mentioned in it. Know that your deeds of wickedness and immorality and your failure to abide by the way of the sons of the Sanūsī do not even require that people tell me about them. You have disobeyed God, the Messenger, and the sons of the Sanūsī in your conduct and actions. I do not approve of you as long as you persist in this way, nor do I consent to your sojourn within our borders; there is no good in proximity to you. The result of the arrival of this my order to you will be, that you leave my country and distance yourselves to some other land that gives you a living, for I will not tolerate sedition and disturbance. As for what you have mentioned concerning people's gossip, that they vilify you in front of me, you, son of whomever you may be, you are one of those people yourself. Knowing this, I give heed to people's talk in regard to your case.

I have warned you and not wronged you. If you go away from our country, that will be better for you; if you do not get up and go, you have wronged yourself.

Farewell.

Year 1328/1910-1911.

1. Triaud, "Relations," p. 1210, note 13.

2. Note that this letter is written in eastern (and not in *maghribī* script); see Document 10, note 1.

3. Spelled as shown.

DOCUMENT 12

Document 12 was written on 2 January 1911 upon the return to Kufra of Muḥammad `Ābid after an extended visit to Cyrenaica. The Sanūsī leader reviewed the correspondence and caravan contacts that had accumulated during his absence and thanked the sultan profusely for continuing to send aid to help Kufra weather the hardships of the deepening drought. The emissary Ibrāhīm al-Gharbī had returned to Kufra and given very favorable reports concerning `Alī Dīnār. Muḥammad `Ābid conceded that some of the activities of the nomads of al-Dōr could not be condoned, and he indicated that `Alī Dīnār was justified in asserting his authority against them.

ويه ثقتى ساشكر نعماك التى لو جحدتها اتر بها حالي ونم بها سري الحمد لله عز
شانه ⁄ بسم الله الرحمن الرحيم وصلى الله على خير خلقه سيدنا محمد مع التسليم ⁄
الى ملجا للاسلام ومضىء الظلام علم الهدى ونجم للاهتدى تاج الجمال واكليل
الكمال العلم المشهور والسميد [1] ⁄ المنصور من جمع من درر الفصاحة اغلاها ومن غرر
البلاغة ابهجها واعلاها ومن جزيل الفضل ارفعه وارقاه و (. . .)[2] ⁄ حيث
استحسنه الله وارتضاه ذى المعارف الفياضة والعوارف الفضفاضة الصادق فى مرضات
رب العلمين العارف ⁄ بالله وحوائج المسلمين الملاذ الاعظم الرءوف الارحم حوطة الاسلام
وحمايته وخديم الدين المحمدي وكنايته مولانا ⁄ وابانا وقرة اعيننا ملجؤنا حيث لا
ملجا ومنعتنا اذ لا منجا من نرغب فى رؤيته ونطلب الله تعالى قوة دولته السلطان ⁄
المعظم مولانا المفخم ظل الله فى ارضه المعتصم بالله تعالى والدنا وسيدنا وسلطاننا
السلطان على دينار ذاك الاسد ⁄ المختار اقر الله بولايته عيون الاسلام وسر بسعيد

ملكه الخاص والعام ولا زالت اعلامه منصوره وسيوف عزه / على رءوس مشهوره ءامين <<ءامين ءامين لا ارضى بواحدة حتى اضيف اليها الف ءامين>> وبعد فاننا نقدم تحيات / تقبل الارض بشفاه التعظيم وتمشي على استحياء اجلالا للمقام العظيم وندعوا لذالك الجناب الرفيع بادعية على الوجه / المشروع ونتبعها بالتامين المقرون بالتذلل والخضوع [3] بغاية الادب والاحترام الى ذاك المقام مقام عز الاسلام الذي / شهد له بذالك الخاص والعام فانه تقبيل الايادي الطاهرة ذات المبرات المتكاثرة ادام الله وجودها وقهر عدوها / وحسودها فان ابنكم بخير لو لا شوقه اليكم وما له نظر الا اليكم اطال الله لنا عمركم السعيد بالعز المديد بجاه النبي السعيد[4] / صلى الله عليه وسلم وشرف وعظم وكرم ءامين قد عرفت الحضرة العلية قبل توجهي الى زيارة الجد رضي الله عنه واني / افدته عن وصول خديمه فرج اليه بحول الله متى ما اتى فقد وجهناه يا سيدى فى مصالح من هنا ومن هنا وانه بعد ذالك / يصلكم بحول الله حيث ما لنا ملجا سواك قد ساعدتنا واوليتنا الخير والبر الكثير حتى سخر الله بسبب ذالك الزوررة / المذكورة ومن حين توجهنا الى ان رجعنا بعون الله ٩ فى شوال من سنة ١٣٢٨ الى الرجوع وصلنا يوم ٢٩ صفر الخير راجعين / من التاريخ المذكور والحمد لله على ذالك وما اتينا محلا الا ودعينا لكم فيه وشكرنا معاملتكم فى كل اوان وان سيدنا / لم ينسانا ولا ترك كتابة اسمي فى جواب الاخ معه فانني والله ممنون جدا جدا شاكر لفضلكم ادام الله لى وجودكم وسرني / بتقبيل اياديكم شناها بحول الله عن قريب انه سميع مجيب ثم انى اتصلت برقيم سيدي الوالد المؤرخ فى ٢٩ ج ل صحبة سيدي / ابراهيم مع ما معه من الهدية الكاملة فقد سرنا ذالك والله سرورا لا يوصف وشكرنا فعلكم الكامل يا سيدي مقبول امركم وما / ترسلوه ما لنا محل غير محلكم وسيدي ابراهيم وصل سالما بما معه واثنى عليكم ثناء لا يوصف

فالحمد لله كيف لا وانتم اليوم / ما فيه محل اسلام غيركم الله يزيدكم كمالا واجلالا ثم ان الجواب ايضا الذي فيه كيفية اهل الدور وما هم فيه اتصلنا / به وقراناه صحبته فالله يهديهم فكتبوا لهم ويكونوا تحت نظركم اولى ان هداهم الله قد تعبوا وفنت ارواحهم فى غير / ما يصلح والله الهادي قد راينا وسمعنا ما هناك محلا غير محلكم اليوم فالحمد لله على ذالك يا سيدي ربنا يزيد فى عمركم // لنا وللاسلام الذين ما لهم سواكم غربا وشرقا وابنكم هذا والله انه فى (غايت)[5] الخجل معكم يسترحم من الحضرة الحنونة (. . .)[2] ان تسامحه وان تكن منه ببال كما هي / عادتها معنا ادام الله وجودها وقهر عدوها وحسودها ابطانا عليكم يا سيدي فى رد الجوابات والتعريف وارسال المذكور فلا تواخذنا فوالله اننا ما / نرتجوا سواكم ويفيدكم بحقيقة الاحوال خديمكم فرج خليفة ها هو بحول الله يصلكم بخير هو ومن معه قاصدين جنابكم راغبين حماكم وانهم ينوبون عنا فى / تقبيل الايادي والاقدام ويسترحمون لنا منكم الرضى والخير وما نوصوكم عليهم وانهم يرجعون سريعا الينا برضاكم وامركم يا سيدي هذا ولا خلافه سوى طلب الخير / والعفو والسماح منكم يا سيدي وشرفونا بخدمتكم وامركم وعرفونا مع كل وافد يا سيدي ودمتم لنا بخير واني اخص الحضرة العالية على الدوام باتم سلام ودمتم / بخير والسلام ابنكم الحقير عبد ربه محمد عابد الشريف / سنه ١٢٢٩ فاتح العام السعيد اعاده الله على الجميع بالعز والرضى ءامين / قلت يا سيدى <<ومثلك من يعفوا ويصفح محسنا لمثلي والاحسان داب الاماثل>>

المتفىء بالفو

القدوسي محمد

ابن السيد الشريف

السنوسي

سنه ١٢٢٠

In Him I trust. "I will give thanks for Your favor, which, even if I disavowed it, my condition would acknowledge, and of which my innermost self would give evidence." Praise be to God; to Him be power.

In the name of God, the Merciful, the Compassionate. The blessings and peace of God upon the best of His creation, our lord Muḥammad. To [him who is] a refuge for Islam, who illuminates the darkness, banner of the true religion, the lodestar of guidance, the crown of beauty, the tiara of perfection, the famous luminary, the proud victorious one, he who has composed the most precious pearls of sophisticated speech and the most splendid and elevated highlights of eloquence, the highest and superior one of those who have many merits, since God found pleasure in him and was pleased with him, who possesses bountiful wisdom and ample knowledge, faithful in the acceptance of the Lord of the Universe, who thoroughly knows God and the needs of the Muslims, the most illustrious refuge, the most merciful of the compassionate, the provident care and protection of Islam, servant of the religion of Muḥammad, and [a supporter] who is sufficient for it, our master and father, the delight of our eyes, our recourse when there was no refuge, our stamina when there was no escape, whom we crave to see, and for the power of whose realm we beseech God Most High, the revered sultan, our honored master, the shadow of God upon His earth, he who takes refuge in God Most High, our father, our lord, and our sultan, Sultan `Alī Dīnār, that chosen lion. May God confirm him in his governance, the fountainhead of Islam, in whose auspicious rule high and low rejoice. May his banners never cease to be victorious and the swords of his might upon necks be illustrious. Amen, amen, amen. "I will not be content with one until I add to it one thousand." Amen.

Thereafter: We offer salutations which kiss the earth with lips of exaltation, and go in deference out of reverence for [your] high rank. We appeal therefore to [your] lofty eminence with legitimate supplications, and we follow it with "amens" combined with self-abasement and humility, with the utmost decorum and respect toward that dignity, seat of the might of Islam, to which high and low testify. [This means] kissing the pure hands possessed of a multitude of good deeds. May God prolong their presence and vanquish those hostile and envious. Your son is well, though longing for you. He looks only toward you. For our sakes may God prolong your auspicious life, with extensive power through the influence of the blissful prophet. May God bless him and grant him peace, distinction, might and nobility. Amen.

I informed [your] eminent majesty before my departure to visit [our] ancestor,[6] may God be pleased with him, and notified [you] that [your] servant Faraj would come to [you] whenever, through the power of God, he might arrive . We have sent him, O master, on matters involving various places. In due course he will arrive before you, through the power of God, for we have no refuge save you. You have aided us, and treated us with such goodness and numerous acts of charity that God has turned these inclinations to profitable account.[7] From the time we left until we returned with the aid of God [on] 9 Shawwāl in the year 1328/14 October 1910--we arrived [at grandfather's] on 29 Ṣafar *al-Khayr*[8] /12 March 1910, while we returned on the previously-mentioned date. Praise be to God for that. Everywhere we went we prayed for you and at all times we gave thanks for your way of dealing with us. Our master has not forgotten us, and did not neglect to have my name written in the letter of the brother with him, for, by God, I am most extremely grateful and appreciative of your generosity. May God lengthen your presence for my sake, and gladden me with [an opportunity] soon to kiss your hands in person, through the power of God, Who hears and answers.

Furthermore, I received via Sīdī Ibrāhīm,[9] the letter of my lord and father dated 29 J.[umāda al-awwa)L. [1328]/8 June 1910 together with the perfect present he brought. That gave us, by God, pleasure that defies description. We gave thanks for your perfect act. O my lord, we accept your order and your letters. We have no place other than yours. Sīdī Ibrāhīm arrived safely with what he brought with him. He extolled your praises in terms defying description. Praise be to God! How could it be different, since these days there is no place of Islam except for you. May God increase your perfection and distinction.

Furthermore, [your] letter also concerns the status of the people of al-Dōr, and their situation. We contacted them and we wrote to them through him

[Ibrāhīm]. We are writing to them that they should more appropriately be under your oversight.[7] May God guide them. They have grown tired and their spirits have faded in the absence of what promotes order. God is the Guide. We have seen and heard that today there is no place there except for yours. Praise be to God for that.

O master, may Our Lord increase your years, for us and for [the followers of] Islam, for whom there is no one like you west or east. By God, this son of yours is extremely embarrassed before you. He asks kindly from your kindhearted majesty . . . that [you] forgive him and think of him as is [your] custom with us, may God lengthen [your] presence and defeat [your] enemies and enviers. We were slow, O master, in replying to your letters, in notifying [you], and sending [you] the above-mentioned [message], but do not blame us, for by God you are our only hope. Your servant Faraj Khalīfa will inform you of the truth of the situation. He will come to you safely, through God's power. He and those with him are coming to you and desire your protection. They act as our deputies in kissing [your] hands and feet, and they kindly ask you for us acceptance and goodness. We do not give you instructions concerning them, for they will be returning quickly to us with your permission and by your command.

O my lord, that is all, except to ask you, O my lord, for goodness, pardon and tolerance. O my lord, honor us with your [requests for] service and your command, and write to us with every envoy. O my lord, for our sake may you remain well. I favor [your] eminent majesty continually with the most perfect greetings. May you remain well. Farewell. Your humble son, the servant of his lord, Muḥammad `Ābid al-Sharīf. The year 1329, the opening day of the fortunate year [1 Muḥarram 1329/2 January 1911]. May God cause it to return with power and favor for all. Amen. O my lord, I have said:

"Like you is he who forgives, and graciously pardons someone like me,
For good deeds are the habit of the exemplary."

Illuminated with ther Most Holy Light

Muḥammad b. al-Sayyid al-Sharīf al-Sanūsī

Year 1320/1902-1903

1. Conjectural reading. A puzzling `*ayn* follows *al-samīd*, possibly, but not evidently, part of the lacuna below it.

2. Lacuna.

3. Reading ḍ for ṣ.

4. Reading *al-sa`īd* for *asa`īd*.

5. Lacuna, conjectural reading.

6. Muḥammad `Ābid probably refers to the grave of the Grand Sanūsī, his father's brother, in Jaghbūb.

7. Conjectural translation.

8. *Al-khayr*: a common epithet of the month of Ṣafar.

9. Probably Ibrāhīm al-Gharbī.

DOCUMENT 13

In Document 13, written in Kufra on 16 March 1911, Aḥmad al-Sharīf addressed `Alī Dīnār formally on behalf of the brotherhood. The head of the Sanūsiyya thanked the sultan for his kind treatment of the nomads of al-Dōr following the problems of the previous year; the opening of the fertile granary province of Dār Masālīt was particularly appreciated. He noted with approval the favorable reports concerning `Alī Dīnār filed by Abū Bakr al-Ghadāmsī, the head of the Sanūsī *zāwiya* in al-Fāshir; had he been less tactful, he might have added that the ambassador's impressions of the king, like those held by the nomads of al-Dōr, had improved dramatically since the crises of 1910.[1] Aḥmad al-Sharīf reported on the status of a consignment of ammunition that Sanūsī agents had purchased for `Alī Dīnār and were now in the process of delivering, and he gave instructions concerning the disposition of a Sanūsī venture in the south. The letter was accompanied by presents, including not only a bandoleer and horse trappings conventional to gift exchanges among kings, but also books, which form of treasure both leaders, though fated to live in violent times, deeply valued. Finally, and beyond its polite rhetorical flourishes, Aḥmad al-Sharīf's letter is perhaps the clearest statement of the Sanūsī brotherhood's sense of affectionate solidarity with, and reliance upon, Sultan `Alī Dīnār of Dār Fūr.

بسم الله الرحمن الرحيم / حضرة ذى المكارم الفياضه والمحاسن الفضفاضه والشمائل
المعطاره والسحائب الجودية المدراره فى المجد / السامى والكرم النامى من همته امضى
من الصارم وعزيته خاضعة لها جميع العزائم واقامت الانام فى ظل وامن / وتركت
الذين يرعى مع الشاء فى كل سهل من الارض وحزن الفاضل الابر مولانا السلطان على
دينار ابن السلطان / فضل ادام الله سعادة ايامه وجعل البسيطة قبض يديه وطوع

احكامه ولا زالت الامال تؤم قصده والاثال / تنتجع غوره ونجوه ءامين وبعد اهداء ما يليق بسنى المقام من اعطر التحية والسلام فان الموجب / له السوال عن تلك الذات المتحلية باجمل الصفات ادام الله علاها وجعل من تقواه حلاها وقد تقدم / منا للحضرة كتاب قبل هذا للسوال عنكم وفيه ما يغنى عن الاعاده وقد ذكرنا لكم من جهة الامانة انها / ان شاء الله قريبة الوصول الى هذا الطرف ونرسلها للحضرة على احسن حال وقد قدم الينا بعض اخواننا / المجابره القادمين من الطرف السعيد[2] ومن الاخوان فى الدور ومعهم اجوبة من اهل الدور والجميع اثنى على / الحضرة بجميل الثنا ففرحنا بذلك ودعونا للجناب بالادعية الرافعة السنا واخبرونا بانكم فتحتم الدرب / على المساليت وعلى الدور وامرتم واوصيتم على من اراد المير من الغلة وغيرها فجزاكم الله احسن الجزا / وقد شكرنا فعلكم وهذا هو المتطوع به عليكم وهذا من الاعانة فى الجهاد لاعلاء كلمة رب العباد فالله تعلى / يبقى وجودكم ويعينكم على ما انتم بصدده من الاقامة بالعباد وتسديد امرهم الى سبيل الرشاد فان اعداء / الله قد عاثوا وتشتتوا فى المسلمين وانبثوا فالمامول من السيادة ان تكونوا يدا واحدة مع الدور وما / دونها وتكون بينكم رابطة الوداد على الدوام كما جمعتكم فى الدين اخوة الاسلام والله تعلى يقول انما المومنون / اخوة فاصلحوا بين اخويكم واتقوا الله وقال صلى الله عليه وسلم لا يومن احدكم حتى يحب لاخيه ما يحب لنفسه / نسئله تعلى ان يسمعنا عنكم ما يسر ويديم راحتكم ويخلد فى العالمين ذكركم وينصركم على عدوكم ءامين ولا زلنا / داعين لكم بالدعوات الصالحه وقاء الليل واطراف النهار ومنا اتم السلام وازكاه وانماه يهدى لمن لاذ بالمقام من الانجال / الكرام واخوتنا جميعا والسيد احمد الريفى يهدون للجناب اكرم التحيه والدعوات الخيريه / والسلام /

حرر ١٥ فى ربيع اول / سنه / ١٣٢٩ //

المقتبس النور

القدوسى احمد ابن

السيد الشريف

السنوسى

١٢٢١

والله اننا فى غاية ⁄ الفرح بكم لانه الان ليس ⁄ هناك محل يعتمد عليه فى ⁄ نصرة الاسلام غير محلكم والا ⁄ عانه بالخوت كالاعانه ⁄ بالاسلحه حتى كادت ⁄ ذواتنا ترقص طربا من ⁄ صنيعكم الجميل وفضلكم الكامل ⁄ هكذا تفعل ملوك الاسلام ⁄ الصادقين بارك الله فيكم ⁄ وجزاكم احسن كما ان اخانا ⁄ الشيخ ابو بكر كتب لنا ⁄ ويقول ان الراحه والخير ⁄ الذى رايته من مولانا [3] ⁄ السلطان ما رايتها ⁄ حتى من والدى فانى فى ⁄ راحهة عظيمه معلا يعلمها الله جزاه الله ⁄ احسن الجزا نعم ونحن ⁄ ان شاء الله لم نزل ساعون ⁄ فى الذى ينوبكم من الجبخانه ⁄ ولو كان ماية الف والتى ⁄ ارسلتم تمنها من سابق ⁄ قضيت حاجتها وتحضر ⁄ فى هذه الايام ان شاء الله ⁄ والله يسهل كل امر بخير ⁄ وبعد كتابة الجواب حضرة ⁄ الامانه ولله الحمد وهى ⁄ اربعه حمول فى ثلاثة ⁄ عشر الف وثلاثه ءالاف ⁄ عدس ومعها اربعه ⁄ من الابل انما زاملتان ⁄ منها ما وصلتا للكفره ⁄ قريبتا العدم فبعناهما ⁄ وكرينا بثمنهما كما هو ⁄ مبين فى التائمه وهذا النوشيك فى غايه من ⁄ الحسن ورخيص لانه ⁄ ارسلنا عليه من محله ⁄ واطلاعكم عليه كفايه // وتتصل اليكم هذه الامانه مع ولدنا على بن بشير ⁄ وولدنا سعيد اوصلهم بحال الصحة والسلامه ⁄ الى ذالك الطرف السعيد نعم والواصل لكم على ⁄ وجه البركة كتاب كشف الغمه وما ارسلناه الا تفاولا ⁄ به نرجوا الله ان يجعل على يدكم كشف غمة هذه ⁄ الامه وايضا ركاب محمر تفاولا بركوب العز

وثلاثه / عذارات حرير وصرع حرير تفاولا ان يجعل / على يدكم صرع العدو الاثين
وكتاب [4] السيره / الحلبيه سيرة النبي صلى الله عليه وسلم جعل الله / سيرتكم على
لهج سيرته صلى الله عليه وسلم والله يبشرنا / عنكم بنصركم على عدوكم وظفركم
بمرادكم نعم وامانه / الحاج عبد الله البشارى التى بطرفكم اذا تيسر امرها / يكون
تسليمها للقادمين اليكم والامر امركم والنظر / لكم والله سبحانه وتعالى يبارك فيكم
وفى ذريتكم / ويجعل منكم قرة العين والسلام يعمكم فى البدء والختام /

In the name of God, the Merciful, the Compassionate. [To] him who possesses bountiful noble virtues, abundant good qualities and perfumed characteristics, who has clouds of liberality pouring forth sublime glory and waxing kindness, whose ambition is keener than the sharp [knife], before whose determination all other wills are humbled, who settled mankind in protection and security and left in peace those who tend the flock in the gentle and rugged areas of the earth, the eminent one of most outstanding piety, our master, Sultan `Alī Dīnār, son of Sultan Faḍl.[5] May God prolong the happiness of his days and put the world in the grasp of his hands and in obedience to his rulings. May hopes never cease to be in concord with his aspirations and may the highborn not cease to seek shelter in his depths and heights. Amen.

After the bestowal of most fragrant salutations and greetings appropriate to [your] sublime position, the purpose of it is to inquire about this personality adorned with the most beautiful characteristics. May God prolong its loftiness and make of his godliness its embellishment.

There has already come to [your] majesty a letter before this one to inquire about you, containing that which need not be repeated. We have mentioned to you in regard to the consignment that it will soon arrive here, God willing. We will dispatch it to [your] majesty in the best of conditions. Some of our *ikhwān*, the Majābra arriving from the southern side, have reached us, and *ikhwān* from al-Dōr. They had letters from the people of al-Dōr, all of whom praised [your] majesty very highly. We were very happy about that, and we said for [your] excellency prayers to enhance your splendor. They also gave us the news that you have opened the road to the Masālīt and al-Dōr, ordering and charging those who want provisions of grain and the like [to use that road]. May God reward you with the best of rewards. We praised your deed. This is something which will be held in your favor, and constitutes support for the *jihād* to make the Word of the Lord of Believers supreme. May God Most High prolong your presence and aid you in that in which you are engaged by way of aiding the believers and guiding their affairs to the path of integrity.

The enemies of God have created havoc, and swarmed out and scattered among the Muslims. It is to be hoped that [your] majesty will act in unison with al-Dōr and not without it. May there be a perpetual bond of affection between you, for the brotherhood of Islam unites you in religion. God Most High says: "The believers are but a single brotherhood: so make peace and reconciliation between your two (contending) brothers; And fear God."[6] [Muḥammad], may God bless him and grant him peace, said: "No one of you is a believer until he desires for his brother that which he desires for himself." We ask [God] Most High that we may hear about you that which gives joy. May he make your repose last, immortalize your name throughout the universe, and give you victory over your foe. Amen.

We never cease to pray for you with pious supplications by day and by night. From us come the most perfect, pure and numerous greetings, to him from among the noble offspring who seeks refuge with [your] noble presence. All our brothers and Sayyid Aḥmad al-Rīfī offer [your] excellency the most noble of salutations and best of prayers. Farewell. It was written on the fifteenth of Rabī` I in the year 1329/16 March 1911.

He who has acquired the Most Holy Light

Aḥmad b. al-Sayyid al-Sharīf al-Sanūsī

1321/1903-1904

By God, we are very happy with you, for these days there is no place except yours there upon which one can depend for the support of Islam. Aid through fraternal assistance is like aid through weapons, so that our hearts are on the verge of dancing in raptures of joy at your good deeds and your consummate kindness. Such are the deeds of truly Islamic kings. May God bless you and reward you with the best. Thus our brother Shaykh Abū Bakr wrote to us saying: "The ease and goodness that I saw from our lord the sultan I never saw before even from my father, for truly I am in splendid, magnificent repose. May God know this, and may He recompense him with the best of rewards."

Yes indeed. If God wills, we will keep up our efforts with regard to what you periodically need in the way of ammunition, even if it be one hundred thousand [rounds]. As for that for which you sent the price previously, I have completed arrangements for it and it will come soon, if God wills, for He provides well for everything.

After the writing of the letter the consignment came, God be praised. It consists of four loads of 13,000 and 3,000 rounds,[7] and with it four camels. However, two burden animals did not reach us in Kufra, for they were close to death. So we sold both, and hired [animals] with the price, as is indicated in the ledger. This bandoleer is extremely beautiful and cheap, because we procured it from its place [of origin]. Your inspection of it will be enough [to convince you of this]. This consignment is coming to you with our son `Alī b. Bashīr and our son Sa`īd. May [God] deliver them in health and safety to that southern side.

Yes indeed. There is coming to you for blessing's sake the book *The Removal of Affliction*,[8] we only sent it as a good omen. We hope that God will enable you to remove the affliction from this nation. Also [coming to you are] reddened stirrups as a good omen to ride with pride, three silk cheekpieces of a horse's harness and a rein of silk, as a good omen that [God] may put into your hand the bridle of the foolish foe. [Also coming to you is] a book, *al-Sīra al-Ḥalabiyya*,[9] a biography of the prophet, may God bless him and grant him peace. May God let the course of your life follow the course of his [the prophet's] life, may God bless him and grant him peace. May God bring us the good news of your victory over your enemy, and may He aid you in attaining what you desire.

Yes indeed. The consignment of al-Ḥājj `Abd Allāh al-Bishārī which is on your side, if you find it convenient, hand it over to those who are coming to you. But the command is yours and oversight lies with you. May God Most High, praise be to Him, bless you and your descendants, and make you the delight of the eye. May peace enfold you at the beginning and the end.

1. Triaud, "Relations," pp. 845-846.

2. Spelled as shown.

3. This word is followed by *alif, lām, sīn*, probably a dittography of the first three letters of the next line.

4. Reading *kitāb* for *kibāb*.

5. `Alī Dīnār is not the son, but the grandson of Sultan Faḍl.

6. Qur'ān, Chapter 49, verse 10. The translation is by A. Yusuf Ali, *The Holy Qur'an: Text, Translation and Commentary* (Brentwood, Maryland: Amana Corp., 1983).

7. The term used is *'adas*, literally meaning "lentils." Lentils would obviously not be counted!

8. Probably the *Kashf al-ghumma 'an jamī` al-umma* of Abū'l-Mawāhib al-Sha`rānī (Carl Brockelmann, *Geschichte der Arabischen Litteratur* (Berlin: Emil Felber, 1898-1902), II, p. 337.

9. *Al-Sīra al-Ḥalabiyya*, a biography of the Prophet by Nūr al-Dīn al-Ḥalabī (975-1044 CE). See A.F.L. Beeston, T.M. Johnstone, R.B. Serjeant and G.R. Smith, eds., *Arabic Literature to the End of the Umayyad Period* (Cambridge: Cambridge University Press, 1983), p. 357; Houtsma, *Encyclopaedia of Islam*, IV, p. 443; and Brockelmann, *Geschichte*, II, 307.

DOCUMENT 14

Document 14 was written in Kufra on 15 January 1912, not long after news of the outbreak of the Italo-Turkish War reached Sanūsī headquarters. Aḥmad al-Sharīf expressed special appreciation to `Alī Dīnār: "these days there is not a king on the face of the earth except for you." He reported that since the Italian invasion of the preceding months had blocked the normal conduct of commerce at the Mediterranean coast, a large shipment of `Alī Dīnār's ivory had been exchanged for ammunition in Kufra itself rather than sent north. A shipment of specie from Dār Fūr, possibly the one requested in Document 10, had arrived safely in Kufra. Aḥmad al-Sharīf asked `Alī Dīnār to expedite the return to Libya of Sanūsī brethern in Dār Fūr, and he requested a present of three pretty slave girls. Finally, the letter announced the death of the elderly Sanūsī leader Aḥmad al-Rīfī, and emphasized the dying man's bestowal of legitimacy and authority upon Aḥmad al-Sharīf.[1]

بسم الله الرحمن الرحيم   حضرة عالى الهمه مشرف الراى فى كل مدلهمه ذى الهمة التى
لا تخبو والمحاسن التى لا تنبو حضرة / السلطان على دينار ابن السلطان فضل ابن
السلطان زكرياء لا زالت ايامه مواسم ولياليه (مباسم) [2] / عامين وبعد اهداء
تحيات عاطره وتسليمات زاهره الى المقام الذى يجب احترامه و (يتاكد) [2] /
اعظامه فان الموجب له السوال عن تلك المكارم التى هى لزهر الربا كمائم ادام الله علاها
/ وجعل من تتواه حلاها وقد تتقدم للحضرة منا كتب قبل هذا وفيها ما يغنى عن
الاعاده وذكرنا / للجناب فى الاخير وصول القادمين من الطرف السعيد وان الامانة
التى ارسلتموها لحضرتكم على / يد صنونا السيد محمد عابد قضاها بهذا الطرف
لتعذر قضائها فى المهاجر البحريه باستيلاء عدو (الله) [2] / الطليان عليها وهم الان سعه

نى محاربة ومحاصره والله يعز الاسلام ويهلك الكفرة (اللئام)[2] ⁄ والقادم الى الطرف السعيد الاخ غيث يخبركم بالاحوال شفاها وعسى بقية اخواننا الذين ⁄ هناك على وصول الينا فلا تحتاج مراحمكم الشريفه الى التاكيد على ارسالهم الينا والله تعلى ييسر ⁄ كل امر عسير ويسمعنا عن الحضرة ما يسر ولا زال الدعاء منا لذلك الجناب مبذولا والله يتولاه (. . . .)[3] ⁄ مقبولا ومنا اتم السلام وازكاه وانماه يهدى لمن حواه المقام من الانجال الكرام ومن (عندنا)[2] ⁄ صنونا السيد محمد عابد والسيد محمد ادريس والسيد محمد رضا وكافة الاخوه يهدون للحضرة كامل التحية والدعوات (الخيرية)[2] ⁄ والسلام تاريخ ٢٥ محرم (الحرام)[2] ⁄ سنه ⁄ ١٢٢٠ //

للمقتبس النور
التدوسى احمد ابن
السيد الشريف
السنوسى
١٢٢١

وقد تقدم لحضرة جانبكم كتاب ذكرنا لكم فيه العزاء ⁄ على استاذى وملاذى سيدى ومولا وقطب ⁄ محياى وواسطتى عند استاذى ووسيلتى ⁄ الى رسولى ومولاى سيدى السيد احمد الريفى ⁄ رضى الله عنه وارضاه وانالنا رضاه بحرمة ⁄ حبيبه ومصطفاه صلى الله عليه وسلم وشرف ⁄ وعظم وكان ابتداء المرض الذى توفى فيه ⁄ ليلت الثلاثا ٤ رمضان المعظم وفى صبحيه ⁄ ذالك اليوم بعد طلوع الفجر ارسل لى ولما ⁄ دخلت عليه وصبحت عليه بالخير قال لى ما ⁄ خفت الا ان يصي بى شىء وانت غايب ⁄ ثم اوصانى بما اراد وفى يوم الاحد ٩ رمضان لما ⁄ جئت لصلاة الصبح

وجدته جالسا فصبحت / عليه وقبلت يده الشريفه وصلينا الصبح وبعد / ها
اضطجع وجلست عند راسه قليلا ثم خرجت / وفى الضحى رجعت وجدته فى النزع الى
قرب / الظهر ففارقت الروح ذالك الجسد العظيم / وتلقاها الملك المامور بالترحيب
والتعظيم / رضى الله عنه وارضاه وجعل الفردس[4] منزله / ومثواه فعظم الله لنا ولكم
فيه الاجر والبركه // ان شاء الله فى اولاده / وقد اجازنى ولله الحمد / اجازة تامه
مطلقة / عامه قايلا لى اجزتك / بجميع ما اجازنى به / الاستاذ رضى الله عنه / بكل
ما يصح له و (عنه)[2] / واسمعنى المسلسلات / وصافحنى وشابكنى / وناولنى
السبحه و [5] / واخذت عنه ولله / الحمد علوما جمه / وفنونا تمه جزاه / الله عنا
وعن كافة / امة محمد صلى الله عليه / وسلم خيرا نعم وما / ارسلتموه لنا وله / من
الدراهم وصل / وبالقبول اتصل / وما قصر تم لا سابقا / ولا لاحقا فجزاكم / احسن
الجزاء واثابكم / من فيض فضله بما / تقر به الاعين يوم / الجزاء ثم المطلوب من /
مكارمكم بمجرد وصول / الجواب اليكم / ان توجهو لنا ولدنا // احمد العايريه
وولدنا بشيرا فاننا فى غاية / الانتظار لهم فالله يديم بقاءكم ويقهر / اعداءكم ويمحى
بسيفكم رقاب الطايفه / الكافره الخاسرة الماكره فان الكفر قد عم / وطم ولم يكن
اليوم ملك على وجه الارض / غيركم فقد اعربتم الدين وقهرتم الملحدين / يجزاكم الله
احسن الجزاء ثم المطلوب من / مكارمكم ان ترسلوا لنا مع الاخ غيث / ثلاثه جوار
جميلات فاحسانكم عام وما / كان منكم التقصير ولا يكون والسلام يعم / جنابكم
والانجال الكرام فى البدء والختام /

In the name of God, the Merciful, the Compassionate.

To the presence of him who is lofty of aspiration, noble of view, who in [every] gloomy [situation] displays a zeal that does not die out, and good qualities that do not go away, his majesty Sultan `Alī Dīnār, son of Sultan Faḍl,[6] son of Sultan Zakariyā'. May his days continue to be festive and his nights smiling. Amen.

After the bestowal of fragrant salutations and flowering greetings to the eminence who commands respect and whose greatness is confirmed. The purpose of it is to inquire about these noble traits which are perianths for the flowers of the fragrant bushes--may God prolong their ascendance, and make of his godfearingness their sweetness. Your majesty has already received letters from us before this, and their contents do not need repeating. We mentioned to your majesty in the last [letter] the arrival of those coming from the south. [As for] the consignment your majesty sent for yourself by the hand of our twin brother Sayyid Muḥammad `Ābid, he has disposed of it here, for it is impossible to dispose of it in the settlements of the coast, because of their conquest by God's enemy the Italians. At present they are engaged in war and blockade with him. May God strengthen Islam and destroy the vile unbelievers! The one who is coming to the south, Brother Ghayth, will inform you of the situation orally. It would be appropriate if the rest of our brethern who are there were to come to us. Nothing is needed from your noble mercy except for reassurance that they will be dispatched to us. May God Most High make easy every difficult matter, and make us hear about your majesty that which gives joy. May our prayers for [your] excellency never cease, and may He arrange for [ ] to be accepted. From us come the most complete, purest, and numerous greetings for those among the noble offspring who belong to your high station. Here our twin brother Sayyid Muḥammad `Ābid, Sayyid Muḥammad Idrīs and Sayyid Muḥammad Riḍā and all the brothers offer to [your] majesty perfect salutations and benevolent prayers. Farewell. The date is 25 Muḥarram *al-Ḥarām*[7] in the year 1330/15 January 1912.

He who has acquired the Most Holy Light

Aḥmad b. al-Sayyid al-Sharīf al-Sanūsī

1321/1903-1904

Your majesty has already received a letter in which we told you about the mourning for my teacher and my refuge, my lord and master, the focal point[8] of my existence and mediator with my *ustādh* [Muḥammad b. `Alī al-Sanūsī] and my intermediary to my apostle and master, my lord al-Sayyid Aḥmad al-Rīfī. May God be pleased with him and reward him, and give us His favor through the sanctity of his beloved and chosen one, may God bless him and grant him peace, and give him honor and greatness. The beginning of the illness from which he died was on the Tuesday night, the fourth of Ramaḍān *al-Mu`aẓẓam*[9] /[29 August 1911]. On the morning of that day, after sunrise, he sent for me. When I came in to him and said good morning, he said to me: "I have only been afraid that something would happen to me while you were absent." Then he charged me with what he wanted done. On Sunday the ninth of Ramaḍān/[3 September 1911], when I came for the morning prayer, I found him seated. I said good morning to him, kissed his noble hand, and we prayed the morning prayer. After that he reclined, and I sat for a little while by his head, then went out. In the forenoon I returned, and found him in the throes of death until almost noon. Then the spirit departed that great body, and was encountered by the angel charged with welcoming and elevating [the dead]. May God be pleased with him and reward him, making paradise his home and his resting place. May God increase through him, as well as through his children, if God wills, our reward and blessing, and yours. God be praised, he had already authorized me with a complete authority, unrestricted and general, saying to me: "I give to you authorization over everything over which the *ustādh* [Muḥammad b. `Alī al-Sanūsī]--may God be pleased with him--gave me authorization, with all its rights and duties." He made me listen to the *al-Musalsalāt.*[10] He clasped my hand, gave me the handshake,[11] and handed me the prayer beads. I took them from him, God be praised, and an abundance of knowledge and complete skills. May God reward him well for us, and for all the nation of Muḥammad, may God bless him and grant him peace.

Indeed. The *dirhams* which you sent to us and him have arrived, and have been received. With us you never fall short, past or present. May God give you the best of rewards. May He repay you from the flood of His abundance with that which is a joy to the eyes on the Day of Reckoning.

What is requested from your noble person is that as soon as this letter arrives you dispatch to us our son Aḥmad al-`Āyariyya and our son Bashīr, for we are awaiting them with great anticipation. May God lengthen your existence and give you victory over your enemies. May He with your sword cut the throats of the faction of the depraved, deceitful unbelievers. For truly the unbelievers are pouring in everywhere; these days there is not a king on the face of the earth except for you. You have proclaimed the religion and defeated the apostates; may God reward you with the best of rewards.

What is asked of your noble person is to send to us with Brother Ghayth three pretty slave girls.

Your beneficence is comprehensive and with us you have never, and will never, fall short. May peace embrace your excellency and the most noble offspring at the beginning and the end.

1. A virtually identical account was sent to the Sanūsī agent in Cairo `Abd Allāh Kaḥḥāl; see Triaud, "Relations," pp. 1589 and 1619-1621.

2. Lacuna; conjectural reading.

3. Lacuna; a hole was punched in the paper here.

4. Spelled as shown.

5. Dittography or lacuna.

6. This is incorrect. He was the son of Zakariyā' and the grandson of Faḍl.

7. *al-Ḥarām*: a common epithet of the month of Muḥarram.

8. *Quṭb:* mystical epithet applied by Ṣūfīs to the leading mystic of each generation; pole or mystic axis of the world (Houtsma, *Encyclopaedia of Islam*, IV, p. 684.]

9. *Al-Mu`aẓẓam*: a common epithet of the month of Ramaḍān.

10. *Al-Musalsalāt al-`ashara fi'l-aḥādīth al-nabawiyya*, a work by Muḥammad b. `Alī al-Sanūsī concerning sound and false chains of succession from the prophet Muḥammad; see Klopfer, *Aspekte*, pp. 68-69.

11. *Muṣāfaḥa*: a special handshake under the sleeve of the shaykh, commonly used in the vow of allegiance. See J. Spencer Trimingham, *Islam in the Sudan* (London: Frank Cass, 1965), p. 206.

DOCUMENT 15

Document 15 was written in Kufra during the middle of January 1912 for dispatch to al-Fāshir not long thereafter with a caravan led by Ghayth Bū Qandīl. In it Muḥammad `Ābid restated emphatically the Sanūsī brotherhood's reliance upon `Alī Dīnār, and specifically entrusted to him command over the Sanūsī nomadic organization of the south, al-Dōr. He reported in some detail on the exchange of `Alī Dīnār's large shipment of ivory for ammunition in Kufra, and explained that the Italian invasion made it impossible to send the ivory north for sale at the coast. Some of the ammunition, along with a present of a horse and a register describing the transaction, were sent south; the balance, concerning which the present letter was silent but which was to figure prominently in later Dār Fūr-Kufra relations, remained for the time being at Sanūsī headquarters.

Document 15 exposes in unusual detail some of the typical problems and misfortunes that inevitably befell Sanūsī traders and diplomats in the southlands: one man had been robbed and stood in need of royal charity, after having waited long and in vain for a companion who might have provided adequate security; the nomads of al-Dōr needed to be assured that `Alī Dīnār was authorized to requisition some of their camels for transport, the delay of merchants in the south remaining a major perceived problem; replacements were needed for transport animals that died along the way, and explanations and compensation were due to the sultan in regard to those lost animals that had belonged to him. The present of a gun had little value if ammunition for it could not be supplied; since few Mediterranean imports were available at the moment due to the Italian invasion, it might be necessary to pay `Alī Dīnār partly in cash, or even to return some of his ivory.

بسم الله تعالى وبحمده وصلاته وسلامه على نبيه وعبده ⁄ استخبر الشمس عنكم كلما طلعت واسال الريح عنكم كلما شرعا ⁄ ابيت والشوق يطويني وينشرني فى راحتيه ولا اشكوا له وجعا ⁄ الى الحضرة العالية والمكارم النامية حدقة الوجود وحديقة الجود من نرغب فى مودته ونطلب الله تعالى ⁄ اجتماعي به سلطاننا ومنتهى حبنا من هو غائب عن اعيننا وحاضر فى فؤادنا سيدنا المنصور بالله تعالى حضرة الملك ⁄ السلطان علي دينار ادام الله وجوده وقهر عدوه واكمد حسوده وجمعنا به ءامين ءامين ءامين ⁄ السلام عليكم ورحمة الله وبركاته بعد تقبيل يديكم على الدوام قد اسرنا ما عملتم لاهل الدور وراحتهم فى محل يريح ⁄ مواشيهم بارك الله فيكم هكذا دابكم ربنا يهديهم وها نحن كتبنا لهم مع هؤلاء وقبل هذا لهم خصوصا انهم يكونوا ⁄ عندكم وتحت امركم وان اردنا حاجة نعرفوكم ونعرفوهم تاتنا زوامل او غير ذالك فان العدو احتاط بالجهات كلها خلاء ⁄ محلكم زاده الله عزا مؤبدا وجاها مؤكدا على الدوام وحرسكم بعينه التى لا تنام نعم فان السن المرسولة امانة سيدنا ⁄ وعددها ستة قناطير ونصف سن فيل نعم وصلت وتقييد وزنها ايضا عندكم اتصلنا بها تماما ومراد سيدنا المنصور بالله ⁄ اضاف جبخانة والعصلى صرفنا عنه النظر كما ذكر سيدنا فما وصلوا خديمكم فرج ومن معه حتى سخر الله حركة الطليان ببني ⁄ غازي وما حصل واهل الوطن فى محاصرة واخبار ذالك ها هو يخبركم به خديمكم غيث بو قنديل وعامر ومن معهم (ان)[1] ⁄ شاء الله وها انا وضعت جوابا لسيدنا ليطلع على اخبار البحر وما حصل فتاملنا واجتهدنا ونظرنا التاخير ربما (. . .)[2] ⁄ حاجة سيدنا حتى تزيل حركت البلاد لانها لا من يدخل ولا من يخرج فيها سالنا التجار الذين بطرننا واخترنا (. . .)[2] ⁄ حاجتكم لانها ابدى من مصالحنا فسخر الله

بيعة عظيمة فى الكفرة وها نحن قيدنا ذالك فى كشف داخل هنا[3] بحضور الذين /
تولوا بيع ذالك وتضاه ولله الحمد بيعة عظيمة وبركة جسيمة فاخذنا ايضا زاملتين
خيرة كذالك مقيد حتهم وهم / ايضا عليهم العدد بالنمرة فى كل صفحة ووجهنا مع
ذالك سيدي غيث محبنا وعامر ورغبنا القادمين من طرفكم نسخر الله / منهم جماعة
ها هم ان شاء الله ياتونكم سيدي وانتم بخير بحول الله وصحبتهم لسيدنا حصان
ابنكم مرادنا تتبلوه منا لوجه / الله وان يكون ناصيت بركته وسرج فخر وعز مؤبد
ان شاء الله يصل سالما ووالله لو هو قلبي ارسله ما لنا جميل فى نعلكم هذا / معنا
ومودتكم لو الدنيا وما فيها ناتيكم بها لكان قليلا يا سيدي وولدكم غيث مراده
وغايته رضاكم وان تنظروا لنا ما / يساعده بالرضى والفرح غيركم يوصى عليه وعلى
هؤلاء ليرجعوا سريعا لاجل نسفر[4] غيرهم كثير بحول الله وكلهم / والله فى فرح
عظيم بكم وحالت بني غازي اضرت بنا عندنا مصالح فيها وفى طرابلس ولم نسمع
حتى الخبر عن ذالك لانه / من ١٠ شوال انتهم الحرابة فى درنة وطبرق
وطرابلس وبني غازي والله يقوي الاسلام ويعليه ولا يعلى عليه // وكنا اردنا توجه
الحاج عبد الله البشاري مع غيث (. . .)[1] هذه المرة و اما غيث ولدكم خديمكم
وخديمنا وجهناه قصدا بامانتكم والحصان اخترنا العجلة لسيدنا / بهذا المتحصل
وفوشيك جبخانة العرابي يتهنى منه سيدنا بحول الله عن قريب ياتيكم وجهناه خديمكم
فرج خليفة فى طلبه هو وحامد بو حليقة وهم يستلمون عليكم / ويطلبون منكم
الفاتحة عن قريب ياتوا به ارسلنا قنطارين ونصف وعجلناهم واليوم هذا لهم قدر ٩
ايام توجهوا واذا ما يوجد بكل تدبير ناتيكم / جنيهات عين بحول الله مع باقي
الزوامل والسن ايضا واما مصروف الابل مع ابلكم حقتنا وفيه جملان ضاعى هنا

تحصل منهم مقدار ٢٥ عاتقية / لانهن ضعاف جدا والبرد صعب على البرية كما يعلم سيدنا نصره الله وعلاه والله المعين وقد استغرب الناس كلهم بيعة السن هذه بالجبخانة اليمان / حالا بثمن فائق والحمد لله كل ذالك من بركة الاسلام وبركتكم واعتنائكم به لا شك ان شاء الله يتم كل ما ترضونه ثم ان جواب سيدنا الذي مع عامر المصري / اسرنا غاية وقبلناه نهاية بحول الله تهنى من كل ما تريده يحضر مضبوطا مجموعا ان شاء الله ليد سيدنا نصره الله وامر البندقة التي من ابنكم لكم والله العظيم / انى فى خجل من تاخر جبخانتها وانها الان لا بد فى البلاد مع عدد وغيرها و (. . . .)[2] وعطر وخياطة هذا ما قدر الله ربنا يريح الاسلام ويفتح البلدان على يديكم / وتاسفنا كل الاسف فى حيازة المصالح هناك وسد الطرق كذالك يا سيدنا راينا اجوبتكم لخديمكم فرج وهو متوجه واعتنائكم وراحته وما ضاع له شيء لله الحمد / خلاف ناقة فى الطريق من زواملكم يعني التي لنا ما هي حقتكم وكلها لكم وتحت امركم والبهيم اعزكم الله كانها عي اتته وتاسفنا عليه لان العيال يريدون يركبون / عليه فان شاء الله فداء عنكم جميعهم ومخلوف بيسطكم وسروركم معنا وما يلزم عرفونا وان بان لكم نظر فى امر بقية السن عرفنا عاجلا ونظركم صواب ونحن / ما عندنا توفق الا حصول جبخانة العرابي ونزيدكم من حق اليونان وتاتي عاجلا والله المعين ءامين وغيث ابنكم غيركم يوصى عليه وفيما يوسع عليه فان / ما تاخر من سابق الا قلة جهده وحصول ما يصلح فى يده والله يطول لنا عمركم ويبيده بعض مصالح يا سيدي ان امكن ارسالها لنا برضاكم وعرفنا اهل الدور وان / تاخذ منهم ٣ او ٤ زوامل تصل وترجع الحاصل ما نريدوا الا بسطكم وراحتكم ومرادنا بحول الله نرسل على جواد لنا بدل هذا ونسعوا فيه فان جاء طيب / (. . . .)[1] هو

لكم ايضا والله يديم علاكم وسامحنا فى قلة ادبنا وتقصيرنا معكم السابق واللاحق كما هو دابكم اطال الله عمركم وحاشاكم تواخذونا او تقصروا معنا / وتنسونا يا سيدي وما ياتونكم سنروهم [4] بما يريدونه سريعا كما هو دابكم فى كل ءان ومع كل احد ان شاء الله على الدوام والاخ غيث يخبركم بجميع الاحوال ان / شاء الله الله يوصلهم بخير جميعا ثم انه فى السابق خديمكم غيث سفر[4] اخوه لجهتكم وكاتبكم متحشم من قلة الجهد وصار منتظر لصنوه متى ما وصل يجهز هو وياتيكم فما سخر الله ذالك / الا توجه (. . .)[2] واداي لان الابل حصل فيها امر تعدي اهل الغزي ام كيف وسيدنا ادرى بحقيقة حالها فها هو طائح عليكم لائذ بكم مسترحم نجدة سيدنا عليه وعلينا ادامكم / الله منجا للانام فدبر والد غيركم يوصى عليه سفروه [4] بدون تامر عليكم سيدنا عاجلا بما نريده ويريده سيدي اطال الله بقاكم واياديكم مقبلات على الدوام / فى كل لمحة ونفس عدد ما وسعه علم الله ءامين ٢٧ محرم سنه ١٢٢٠(١) // ابنكم محمد عابد الشريف / السنوسي // وقيد مصلحات تروه بيد خديم (. . .)[1] // وغيركم يوصى سيدي على خديمكم / غيث ورفقته وانت اعرف / العارفين وسامحونا فى / قلة الادب / معكم

المتضيء بالضو

القدوسى محمد

ابن السيد الشريف

السنوسى

سنه ١٢٢٠

In the name of God Most High, and with praise to Him. His blessings and peace upon His prophet and servant.

"I seek news of you from the sun each time it dawns,
and inquire of the wind about you whenever it arises.
I pass the night, and my longing envelopes me;
It spreads me out in the palms of its two hands,
but I do not complain of pain."

To [your] sublime majesty, [of] ever-increasing noble deeds, the pupil of the eye of being and garden of liberality, whose affection I crave, and with whom I ask God Most High to be united, our sultan, the pinnacle of our love, who is absent from our eyes but present in our heart, our lord, the victorious with God Most High, his majesty the king, Sultan `Alī Dīnār. May God prolong his presence, vanquish his foe, make heartsick the one who envies him, and unite us with him. Amen, amen, amen. Peace be upon you, and the mercy of God, and His blessing.

After kissing your two hands always, we are pleased at what you have done for the people of al-Dōr and their comfort in a place which gives repose to their livestock. God bless you! That is your way, and may Our Lord guide them. We wrote especially to them, this time and before, that they belong to you and are under your rule, and that if we wanted something, we would notify you and notify them so that camels or whatever would come to us. The enemy has closed in from every side except your kingdom. May God increase its power endlessly, and make its esteem forever sure, and protect you with His eye that does not sleep.

Yes indeed.[5] As for the ivory sent by our lord on consignment, its amount was six *qinṭārs* and a half of elephants' teeth. Yes indeed. It arrived. Its weight had been recorded on your side too, and we have received the complete [shipment]. As for the desire of our lord, the victorious with God, [to obtain] additional ammunition and Ottoman [rifles], we have turned our attention to it, just as our lord said. No sooner had your servant Faraj and those with him arrived than God caused the movement of the Italians in Benghazi and what happened [thereafter]. The people of the country are in a state of siege; your servant Ghayth Bū Qandīl and `Āmir and those with them will tell you about that, if God wills. I sent a letter to our lord conveying the news of the sea. We reflected deeply, and we tried hard, but we experienced delay. Perhaps our lord [. . .] business until the land's turmoil ends, for now no one gets into or out of it. We asked the merchants who are with us and we chose [. .] your goods, for they take precedence over our own affairs. God allowed a big sale to occur in Kufra. We recorded that in a register[6] enclosed herein, in the presence of those charged with making the sale and the settlement. Praise be to God, it was a good sale and a great blessing. In similar fashion, we have taken two good camel-loads; their value has also been recorded, their number also having been indicated with the figures on every page. My lord, we have sent our beloved Ghayth and `Āmir with those [goods], and we want people to come from your side. May God put all of them to good use. If God wills, my lord, they will come to you while you are well, through God's power. They will have with them, for our lord , your son's own horse. We would like for you to accept it, for the sake of God. Let it be the forelock of His blessing, and a saddle of everlasting might and power. If God wills, it will arrive safely.

By God, O master, I would even send my heart, so much do we appreciate these acts of yours, and your friendship; I would bring you even the world and everything in it, and that would be little. Your son Ghayth 's only wish and aim is to please you, and that for our sake you watch , with pleasure and joy, for that which helps him.[7] You of all people do not need to be asked to direct him and those [with him] to return swiftly so that we can often send others, through God's power. By God, all are very pleased with you. The situation in Benghazi has hurt us, for we have interests there, and in Tripoli. We have not even heard news from there, for on 10 Shawwāl [1329]/4 October 1911 soldiers came to Derna, Tobruk, Tripoli and Benghazi. May God empower Islam, make it dominant and let nothing dominate it.

We wanted to send al-Ḥājj `Abd Allāh al-Bishārī with Ghayth [ ] this time. As for Ghayth, your son and servant, and our servant, we have sent him for the purpose of [delivering] your consignment. As for the horse, from the yield of this, we have selected a fast one[7] for our lord. A bandoleer of Remington ammunition[8] which should please our master, with God's power, will come to you soon. We have sent your servant Faraj Khalīfa in search of it--him and Ḥāmid Bū Ḥalayqa--and they will hand it over to you and ask the *fātiḥa* from you. They will bring it soon. We have sent two and one-half *qinṭārs* and urged them to hasten; as of today they have been gone nine days. If it is not to be found by any means, you will receive, by God's power, pounds in cash, along with the rest of the burden camels and the ivory too. As for camel expenses, with regard to your camels here with us, the yield from two camels which collapsed here was only an amount of 35 *`ātiqiyyas*[9] because they were very weak, and the cold is hard on living creatures, as is known to our lord. May God grant him victory and raise him up, and God is the Helper. The sale of this ivory under present conditions, for Greek ammunition, at an excellent price, surprised everyone. Praise be to God. All that [came about] through the blessing of Islam, and through your blessing and assistance. Undoubtedly, if God wills, all your wishes will be fulfilled. Moreover, the letter of our lord which came with `Āmir al-Maṣrī cheered us greatly and we accepted it definitively. By God's power, you will enjoy all that you desire. If God wills, it will all together and complete come to the hand of our lord, may God give him victory. [As for] the matter of the gun from your son for you, by the Almighty God, I am embarrassed at the delay of its ammunition. At present there is no way into the country with regard to implements and such things, and [. . .], perfume, and garments. Such is God's decree, but may our Lord relieve Islam and open the lands at your hands. We are extremely sorry about the holding up of business there, and about this blockage of the roads, O master.

We have seen your letters to your servant Faraj, and your help toward his comfort while he was on the way. He did not lose anything on the road, God be praised, except a she-camel from among your burden animals, that is, one of ours and not your property--though all are yours, and yours to command. May God increase your power. The animal seems to have been overcome by fatigue, and we are sorry about that because the children liked to ride it. God willing this sacrifice will result in your pleasure and happiness with us. Inform us of what is needed. Should you have an opinion about how to dispose of the rest of the ivory, let us know quickly, for your opinion is correct [guidance], as we have no instructions except to obtain Remington ammunition, to supplement it for you from the [ammunition] of the Greeks, and that it should come quickly. God is the Helper. Amen.

As for your son Ghayth, others than you will counsel him and [tell him] how to make profit. The only thing that held him back previously was his lack of effort and [the failure] to get hold of that with which to do business. May God prolong your life for our sake. He is in need of some goods, O master; if possible, and with your approval, [please] send them to us. We informed the people of al-Dōr that if you take 3 or 4 burden camels from them, these will go and yield a return. We desire only your pleasure and ease. It was our desire, with God's power, to send for a horse to take the place of this one, and to act quickly. If it comes, fine; it is also for you. May God prolong your eminence. Be tolerant of our lack of manners and our previous and subsequent shortcomings, as is your custom. May God prolong your life. O my lord, God forbid that you blame us, neglect us, or forget us. Send those who come to you away quickly with what they want, as is your custom, if God wills, at any moment and with anybody.

Brother Ghayth will inform you about everything, if God wills. May God make all of them to arrive safely. Moreover, Ghayth your servant formerly sent his brother to you, and he wrote to you apologizing for his lack of enterprise. Then he waited for his twin brother, so that when he would arrive he would get ready and come to you. But God did not make that possible. Instead, he went [.] Wadai, because the camels were despoiled by robbers, is that not so? Our master knows the true state of affairs. Now he throws himself upon your [mercy] and seeks refuge with you, asking for mercy, and for the aid of our master, for him and for us. May God preserve you as a refuge for humanity, and a father. Arrange [for him] a father other than yourself to counsel him.

Send him off at once, O lord, without intimidating him and with whatever I and my lord may desire.

May God lengthen your life, and may your hands always be kissed, with every glance and breath, as many as God's wisdom accommodates. Amen. 27 Muḥarram 1330/17 January 1912. Your son Muḥammad `Ābid al-Sharīf al-Sanūsī. The list of the goods you will see in the hand of [your] servant [.]. Let someone other than you counsel your servant Ghayth and his companions, for you are the most knowledgeable of all those with knowledge. Be tolerant of our lack of manners towards you.

Illuminated with the Most Holy Light
Muḥammad b. al-Sayyid al-Sharīf al-Sānūsī
Year 1320/1902-1903

1. Lacuna, conjectural reading.
2. Lacuna.
3. *Hunā* is written above the line.
4. The *fā'* has the dot above the letter; this is unusual in a letter written in *maghribī* script.
5. *Na`m*, meaning "yes," or "yes, indeed," is commonly used in this correspondence too indicate a transition to another topic. Here is just seems to give emphasis.
6. Fragments of this register survive; they have not been included in this collection.
7. Conjectural translation.
8. *`Arābī:* Remington (Triaud, *Tchad*, p. 114).
9. *`Ātiqiyya*: "la `Atqiya (cotonnade bleue de 7 m. de long)" (Triaud, *Tchad*, p. 67). Le Cheikh Mohammed ben Otsmane el-Hachaichi, *Voyage au pays des Senoussia, à travers la Tripolitaine et les pays Touaregs* (Paris: Challamel, 1903), p. 74 gives: "les cotonnades ordinaires bleues de mauvaise qualité."

DOCUMENT 16

Document 16 was also prepared in Kufra in the middle of January 1912. Muḥammad `Ābid noted the passing of Aḥmad al-Rīfī, and the arrival and disposition of a shipment of coinage belonging to the deceased--probably the sum previously mentioned in Documents 10 and 14. The Sanūsī leader reported the safe arrival of the sultan's caravan, and indicated that it came accompanied by a detailed shipping manifest, which Muḥammad `Ābid's people checked carefully, item by item. The right of `Alī Dīnār to levy camels from al-Dōr was reconfirmed, including some belonging to the son of the Tuareg leader `Abd al-Qādir al-Azraq. Muḥammad `Ābid praised the king highly, describing him as a father to Islam and to the Sanūsiyya. An oblique reference to "the matter of the people of the government" hints that `Alī Dīnār had written to Kufra with some candor concerning his insulting and futile tributary status under Anglo-Egyptian overlordship; the precise message referred to remains unknown.

بسم الله الرحمن الرحيم وصلى الله على سيدنا محمد الشفيع فى امته يوم الجحيم /

الحمد لله ذى الطول والانعام الذي تفضل على عباده بالمصطفى رحمة للانام وامرنا

سبحانه باقتفاء اثر هذا النبي الكريم / الهادي الى صراط النعيم صلى الله تعالى عليه

وسلم وعلى ءاله وصحبه وذريته ما مؤمن قلبه بالشهادة ترنم وبعد فهذا الى حضرة /

الملك الاعظم سلطاننا الافخم من نشر اعلام الهداية بين الانام ونشر الخير محبة ورغبة فى

قوة الاسلام وتوج الناس / وارشدهم بمعرفة جوده فالناس يعترفونه من فيض بحره

وجوده فهو علم السعادة وسبيل الرشاد وزهرة على جبين الزمان / لكل من استفاد

جامع كلمة الايمان وقامع عبدة الاوثان والصلبان سيف الله القاطع وشهاب اللامع الساطع

سلطان / الاسلام والمسلمين ناشر جناح العدل فى العلمين حامي حمى الملة والدين

سلطان سلاطين العالم وناشر لواء العدل ⁄ بين من حارب وسالم سلطاننا سيدنا
السلطان المنصور بالله تعالى محبنا قرة اعيننا سيدنا السلطان علي دينار ⁄ اعلى
الله صيته فى جميع الاقطار بحرمة النبي المختار صلى الله عليه وسلم وجمعنا به وطال
لنا عمره وللاسلام ءامين ⁄ ءامين ءامين ءامين ءامين السلام عليكم ورحمة الله وبركاته
ومغفرته ومرضاته وازكى تحياته وزيادة رحماته تقبل يديكم و (تقبل)[1] ⁄ بين يديكم
لا انقطاع لذالك جمعنا الله بكم فى ابرك وقت ءامين ثم نعرف سلطاننا واعز الناس
عندنا فى ابرك وقت (تشرفنا)[1] ⁄ برقيمكم المحبوب وخطابكم الذي عندنا هو
اعز مطلوب فانشرح الفؤاد وفرح به جميع العباد حيث انكم ولله الحمد ⁄ بخير فى
اعلى الهمة واقين وفى فعل الخير وقوة الاسلام على الدوام راغبين فجميع من معنا
عيالكم اولادنا والاخوان ⁄ داعون لكم بالخير والنصر وزيادة العز والظفر وكان وصول
ابنكم بل خدامكم فرج خليفة فى ءاخر الحجة وكان يوم (وصوله)[1] ⁄ يوم عيد وفرح
وكافة رفقاؤه داعون لكم بالخير شاكرون لاحسانكم الزائد فالحمد لله على ذالك ثم اننا
فى اول (رمضان)[1] ⁄ المعظم حل بنا ما قدره الله لكل ذى روح من انتقال والدنا
الولي الصالح السيد احمد الريفي صبحية ٩ فى رمضان (المعظم)[1] ⁄ قرب نصف
النهار فعظم الله اجرنا واجركم فيه ورزقنا واياكم التوفيق لرضاه كما انه يسلم عليكم
كثيرا ويدعوا لكم بالخير ⁄ فابشر به وانت فيه لا شك هنيئا لكم بذالك يا سيدنا وقد
تاخر الخبر لكم والعزاء كما هو معلوم من قلة من يتوجه (. . .)[2] ⁄ لان اهل
الدور سابقا ربنا يهديهم فالحمد لله قد انحازوا فى راحتهم وراحتنا معكم ربنا يوفقهم
ويجعلهم لاوامركم (ممتثلين)[1] ⁄ راغبين ان ارادوا الخير واننا لا نرضوا منهم

خلانكم ابدا ربنا يجعلكم منجا للانام ومصباحا مضيئا على الدوام ثم نعرف (سيدنا)[1]

/ المنصور بالله ان السن وصلت بتمامها وان الدهن والسكاكين وما معهم وصلني كما

هو متيد فى الكشف حاجة (حاجة)[1] / وتوبل[3] ذالك بالفرح العظيم فربنا يزيد

فى خيركم وعمركم لنا وللاسلام فالحمد لله على ذالك كما ان خديمكم فرج خليفة /

يثني عليكم غاية ويمدح فيكم نهاية ربنا سبحانه وتعالى يقوى مددكم وينصر جيشكم

ويجعلكم ملاذا للقاصدين ورحمة (الكل)[1] / من نظركم او تعرف بكم قد تواترت

علينا مبراتكم وانعاماتكم حتى اثقلتم ظهورنا وعجزنا ان نكافيكم فلا زال بحول (الله)[1]

/ امركم مطاع والدعاء لكم مبذولا والله يتولاه اجابة وتبولا واعلم يا سيدنا تولنا لكم

والدنا ما هى صعبة كيف لا و (انت)[1] / تحق لكم هذه واعظم زادكم الله اجلالا

وتعظيما فى الدنيا والاخرة فهي منا واجبة لحناناتكم علينا ولانكم لهذا (الان)[1] /

للاسلام ابا قد خصكم الله بشيء زادكم الله ذالك انتم تادبتم ما رضيتموها مع الله

ومعنا ونحن واجبة علينا و (قليلة)[1] // حتكم معنا واجوبة سيدنا تاريخها فى ١٢

شعبان و (. . .)[2] ايضا ثم بعدهم فى ٢٠ رمضان المعظم ثم (فى)[1] ٢٤

شوال الجميع اتصلنا بهم مع ابنكم فرج / الا الذي مع عامر اتانا بعدهم بتدره

ايام وهو الذي ٢٤ شوال نعم امر دراهم المرحوم وصلت تماما وسلمناها لولده

احمد ابن ابنه بارك / الله فيكم وفيه وهو يدعي لكم بالخير ويتبل اياديكم هو واخوته

وعامة بيتهم العامر والحمد لله الذي وصلكم وفرحتم به ابنكم فرج وتوجه كذالك (الينا)[1]

/ وهو يثني عليكم ليلا ونهارا شاكرا لنعلكم على الدوام ونحن كذالك وذكر سيدنا

على امر ناسات الحكومة فهمنا ذالك وقبلناه يا سيدنا من يعمل غير (. . .)[2]

/ العمل يا والدنا ربنا يطول لنا عمركم ويديم لنا وجودكم ءامين وسلامنا يخص

سيدنا ومن تعلق به ومن عندنا الاخوة وولدكم محمد الشريف واخوته و (عليكم)[1]
/ منا يا قرة العين اتم سلام والسلام // ابنكم محمد عابد الشريف / السنوسي /
سنه (١)٢٢٠ فيه محرم ٢٧ // سامحونا فى قلة الادب معكم / وعدم
المعرفة لقدركم سيدي / فانتم للشفقة والسماح اهل / سيدى // مبارك هذا العام
الجديد السعيد بكم ويعود عليكم سنينا واعواما / ان شاء الله مبارك مبارك ودمتم
لنا امنين سالمين // ويا سيدنا عرفنا اهل الدور ٤ زواسل سيدي / وثلاثة من
ابن عبد القادر الازرق واوصيناهم / ان يمتثلوا اوامركم زيادة وانتم ان لم يعطونها /
انتم تاخذونها ترسلوها يا سيدنا لنا / اطال الله عمركم ءامين

المتضيء بالضو
القدوسي محمد
ابن السيد الشريف
السنوسي
سنه ١٢٢٠

In the name of God, the Merciful, the Compassionate. The blessings of God upon our lord Muḥammad, intercessor for his community on the day of Hell-fire. Praise be to God, Who possesses might and munificence and Who bestowed upon His worshipers the chosen [prophet], a mercy to mankind. Praise be to God, Who has ordered us to follow the footsteps of this noble prophet, the guide to the path of grace. May God Most High bless him, his family, his companions, and his descendants, and give them peace for as long as the heart of any believer resounds with the profession of faith.

Thereafter: This is to the presence of the most mighty king, our most glorious sultan, who has spread the banners of guidance among mankind and has dispersed benevolence in love and desire for the power of Islam. He has been a crown to the people and has guided them well through knowledge of his generosity, for the people acknowledge him, by virtue of the overflow of his sea of kindness, for he is the badge of happiness and the path of right conduct; he is the bloom upon the forehead of the age, to all willing to benefit. It is he who unites the faithful and subdues those who worship idols and crosses, the sharp sword of God and His brilliantly luminous flame, the sultan of Islam, and of the Muslims, he who spreads the wing of justice throughout the universe, the protector of the community and of religion, sultan of the sultans of the world, who spreads the banner of justice between those at war and those at peace, our sultan, our lord the sultan, victorious with God Most High, our beloved, the joy of our eyes, our lord Sultan 'Alī Dīnār. May God exalt his reputation in all quarters, through the sanctity of the chosen prophet, may God bless him and grant him peace, and unite us with him. May God lengthen his life for our sakes, and for the sake of Islam. Amen, amen, amen, amen, amen.

Peace be upon you, and the mercy of God, and His blessing, forgiveness and acceptance, and His purest salutations, and an abundance of His mercies.

May your hands receive [these], and may they be accepted by you without interruption. May God bring us together with you in the most blessed of times. Amen. We inform our sultan, he who is the most powerful of persons among us, that at the most blessed of times we have been honored by your beloved missive. Your letter which we have [received] was what was most dearly desired. It has gladdened the heart, and has made all the worshipers rejoice for, praise be to God, you are well, a protector with the keenest zeal, and always desiring benevolent acts and the strength of Islam. All with us [here], your children and ours, and the *ikhwān*, are praying for your wellbeing, victory, and increasing power and triumph. The arrival of your son, nay, your servant, Faraj Khalīfa, occurred at the end of [Dhu']l-Ḥijja [29 Dhu'l-Ḥijja 1329/21 December 1911]. The day of his arrival was a day of celebration and rejoicing. All his companions prayed for your wellbeing, giving thanks for your abundant kindness. Praise be to God for that!

Then, at the beginning of Ramaḍān *al-Mu'aẓẓam*[4] there befell us what God has decreed for every living creature, the passing of our father, the devout and saintly Sayyid Aḥmad al-Rīfī, on the morning of 9 Ramaḍān *al-Mu'aẓẓām* at about noon [9 Ramaḍān 1329/3 September 1911]. May God through him enhance our recompense and yours, and through acceptance of him, give us and you success, for he sent greetings to you frequently and prayed for your wellbeing. Rejoice about this, O my lord, for without a doubt there is benefit for you in it. The news about the mourning has been slow in coming to you, as can be understood from the scarcity of travellers [. . .], because formerly the people of al-Dōr....may Our Lord guide them. Praise be to God, they have united to bring relief to themselves and relief to us in regard to you. May Our Lord grant them success and make them obey your commands willingly, if they desire good, for we will never accept that they disobey you. May Our Lord make you ever a refuge for humanity, and a shining light. Thereafter, we inform our lord, the victorious through God, that all the ivory arrived, and that the fat, the knives and what was with them came to me exactly as specified in the register, item by item. That was received with great joy. May Our Lord increase you in prosperity, and also in years, for our sake and for the sake of Islam. Praise be to God for that.

Your servant Faraj Khalīfa too praises you highly and commends you greatly. Praise be to God Most High. May Our Lord strengthen your support, render your army victorious, and make you a refuge for those who strive and a mercy for all who look at you and recognize you. Your good deeds and favors toward us have followed each other in succession, so that you have laden our backs [with favors], while we have been unable to repay you. But with God's power, may your orders continue to be obeyed, and may prayers for you never cease to be offered freely, and may God arrange to answer and accept these [prayers]. O our lord, know that it is not difficult for us to call you our father. Why should it be so? No, you deserve this and more. May God increase your splendor and glory in this world and the next, for this is obligatory upon us in return for your compassion toward us, because at this time you are a father to Islam. God has already bestowed upon you a special quality; may He increase that, for you have cultivated manners that you find pleasing both in regard to God and ourselves. We are under obligation to you, for you have found little reward from us.[5]

The letters of our master dated 13 Sha`bān /9 August 1911 and [ . . ] too, and then after them of 20 Ramaḍān /14 September 1911, then 24 Shawwāl/18 October 1911, all came to us with your son Faraj, except that the one with `Āmir came to us a few days later, and that was the one of 24 Shawwāl. Indeed. As for the matter of the *dirhams* of the deceased, which arrived intact, we have handed them over to his [grand]son Aḥmad, the son of his son. May God bless you and him. He prays for your wellbeing, and he kisses your hands, he and his brothers, their whole numerous family. Praise be to God Who brought your son Faraj to you, and you were pleased with him. Now he has also come to us, praising you night and day and continually thanking you for your deeds--and we do likewise. Our master has mentioned the matter of the people of the government.[6] We have understood that and accepted it, O master. [. . .] O our father, may Our Lord prolong your life for our sake, and preserve your existence. Amen.

Our special greetings to our lord and those associated with him. Here from the *ikhwān*, and your son Muḥammad al-Sharīf and his brothers, to you from us, O delight of the eye, a most perfect greeting. Farewell. Your son Muḥammad `Ābid al-Sharīf al-Sanūsī. 27 Muḥarram [1]330/17 January 1912.

O my lord, please forgive us for our lack of manners with you, and our ignorance of your status, for compassion and tolerance befit you, O my lord. May this happy new year be blessed for you, and if God wills, many blessed returns. For our sake may you remain safe and secure.

O our lord, we have informed the people of al-Dōr about 4 burden camels, my lord, and three belonging to the son of `Abd al-Qādir al-Azraq. We have advised them to obey your orders for more.[7] If they do not give them, then you will take them, and send them on to us, O my lord.

May God lengthen your life. Amen.

Illuminated with the Most Holy Light

Muḥammad b. al-Sayyid al-Sharīf al-Sanūsī

Year 1320/1902-1903

1. Lacuna, conjectural translation.
2. Lacuna.
3. Spelled as shown.
4. Al-Mu`aẓẓam: a common epithet of the month of Ramāḍān.
5. Conjectural translation.
6. Probably this is a reference to the British government.
7. Conjectural translation.

DOCUMENT 17

Document 17 is a final member of the group of letters prepared in Kufra in the middle of January 1912 to be sent to Dār Fūr soon thereafter with the caravan of Ghayth Bū Qandīl. In it the Sanūsī leader `Alī al-Khaṭṭābī thanked the Dār Fūr sultan for the gift of a gun; in the event, it was a favor that `Alī al-Khaṭṭābī would repay many times over before the end.

بسم الله الرحمن الرحيم / انه الى حضرة صفوة الاكارم الامجاد الجامع ما تفرق من مكارم
المحامد بدر المفاخر الذى اضاءت به نواحيها ومنار / المآثر الذى اهتدى به ساريها
الملك الجليل المقتدار سلالة السلاطين الاكرمين مولانا السلطان على دينار / ابن السلطان
زكريا العباسى اعز الله اعلامه وانصاره وضاعف مجده واقتداره ءامين وبعد اهداء
سلام يحقه / من التكريم ما يليق بذلك الجناب العظيم فان الموجب لتسطيره و الباعث
على ابرازه وتحريره السوال عن تلك المكارم / التى هى لزهر الربا كمائم ابقاكم الله
تعلى تاجا لاعالى المعالى وغياثا للرعايا والموالى وان سالتم عن احوال / هذا الطرف
فان جميع من فيه من الاخوة والاخوان ولله الحمد فى دوام المسرات وتمام المبرة
والاحسان مواظبون / على ما تعهد حضرتكم السنيه من الدعوات الخيريه بدوام نصر
مولانا وبقائه وتاييد رجال دولته واوليائه / والبندقة التى جاءتنا من حضرة جنابكم
العالى قد وصلتنا على احسن حال وتوبلت [1] منا بغاية السرور ومزيد / الاقبال
ودعونا الله تعالى رافعين اليه اكف الضراعة والابتهال سائلين منه سبحانه ان يديم
وجودكم / محفوفين بالرعاية والاجلال ويجعل دولتكم المحمية وارفة الظلال سابغة
الانعام والافضال ونرجوا من الله / القبول انه خير مامول واكرم مسئول هذا وسلام

السلام يخصكم و يعم اللائذين بساحة ذالك المقام و (من)[2] / عندنا كافة الاخوان
يهدون لحضرة جنابكم افضل التحيه ويدعون لكم بصالح الادعيه والسلام تاريخ غرة
صفر / سنه / ١٢٢٠ / عبد ربه على الخطابى / ابن السيد محمد الشريف /

الضياء بالضو القدوسى
على ابن السيد الشريف السنوسى
١٢٢٢

In the name of God, the Merciful, the Compassionate.

To the presence of the best of the most noble and illustrious, who unites what was dispersed in regard to noble characteristics and praiseworthy deeds, the full moon of glorious exploits, through whom its regions are illuminated, beacon of glorious deeds, to guide him who journeys through the night, the great and mighty king, offspring of the most noble sultans, our master Sultan `Alī Dīnār, son of Sultan Zakariyā al-`Abbāsī. May God give power to his banners and followers, and redouble his glory and strength. Amen.

After the bestowal of a greeting bordered with tribute appropriate to that honorable and august [monarch], the reason for writing, and the occasion for presenting and composing it, is to inquire about this noble nature, which is like the calyx to the blooms of the hillside. May God Most High keep you and preserve you as a crown for the highest of the high, and a succor for subjects and dependents. If you ask about conditions here, all of the brothers and the *ikhwān* are in continual happiness and perfect kindness and beneficence, praise be to God, diligently applying themselves to what is owed to your sublime majesty in regard to benevolent prayers for the perpetuation of our master's victory, and his preservation, and for the support of the men of his state, and for his guardians.

The gun which came to us from your eminent majesty arrived here in the best of conditions. We have received it with the greatest joy and warmest acceptance.

We pray to God Most High, raising up to Him open palms of entreaty and supplication, asking Him (Praise be to Him) to preserve your existence, surrounded by respect and majesty, and to make your protected state a verdant shade, and abundant in merit and kindness. We hope that God will accept this, for He is the Most Benevolent Fulfiller of Hopes and the Most Generous Answerer of Requests.

Farewell. Greetings for you especially, and for all those who seek refuge at the court of that eminent [lordship]. Here all the *ikhwān* direct toward your eminent majesty the best of salutations, and they pray for you with the most sincere prayers. Farewell. The date is the first of Ṣafar in the year 1330/21 January 1912.

The worshiper of his Lord, `Alī al-Khaṭṭābī b. al-Sayyid Muḥammad al-Sharīf.

Lit with the Most Holy Light
`Alī b. al-Sayyid al-Sharīf al-Sanūsī
1322/1904-1905

1. Spelled as shown.
2. Lacuna, conjectural reading.

DOCUMENT 18

Document 18 was written in Kufra on 22 September 1912. In it, Muḥammad Idrīs responded in vigorous and critical terms to `Alī Dīnār's clampdown upon the refugee Tuareg of al-Dōr and his arrest of their leaders Ṣāliḥ Abū Karīm and `Abd al-Raḥīm Maṭārī. He reminded the Dār Fūr sultan of the sacrifices these refugees had endured during their Hijra out of French-controlled territory, and threatened to sever relations between Kufra and Dār Fūr if they were not released. `Alī Dīnār did release a number of the arrested leaders soon after this letter arrived in al-Fāshir, perhaps at least in part as a response to the sentiments it conveyed. From `Alī Dīnār's perspective, the letter quietly invited him to expell the men he considered troublemakers from Dār Fūr by sending them to the Sanūsī leaders, and that was precisely the course of action he adopted; Ṣāliḥ Abū Karīm, `Abd al-Raḥīm Maṭārī and a number of other detainees were expelled from Dār Fūr by being placed in charge of a large caravan of provisions sent by the king to relieve the beleagured Sanūsī community of Gouro, where a miniscule but timely Ottoman intervention was successfully deterring French occupation. The relief caravan was attacked and looted by the French on 15 May 1913; a number of Sanūsī leaders from the al-Dōr command were killed or captured.[1] Meanwhile, many of the ordinary refugee Tuareg of al-Dōr were not sent back to the Sanūsī leaders, but were resettled under supervision as permanent subjects of Dār Fūr.

بسم الله الرحمن الرحيم / انه من محمد ادريس ابن السيد محمد المهدى ابن السيد
محمد بن على بن السنوسى الخطابى الحسنى الادريسى الى عمدة الكرام / ونخبة
الجهابذة الفخام سليل المعالى حسنة الايام والليالى ذى الهمم الساميه والمكارم الناميه
غاية الامال و (. . .)[2] / السداد والكمال السلطان الفاضل ابن السلطان الكامل

حضرة السلطان على دينار ابن السلطان فضل العباسى / ادام الله اجلاله و بلغه من خير الدارين ءاماله وسدد اقواله وافعاله وبعد اهداء ما يليق بسنى المقام من اعطر / التحايا الدائمة الانسجام فان الموجب له السوال عنكم وعن ما انتم عليه من الاحوال جعلها الله احوال رضى / بحرمة النبى المرتضى صلى الله عليه وسلم وشرف وعظم وان تفضلتم بالسوال عنا فان جميع من بالطرف من الاخوان فى خير / وعافيه ونعم ضافيه نرجوه تعلى ان تكونوا كذلك على الدوام بجاه النبى عليه الصلاة والسلام هذا وليكن فى شريف / علمكم انه من مدة سنة او سنتين قد عدى عدو الله الفرنصيص على جهة الدور واستاصل من فيه والاخوان الذي هناك / منهم من مات ومنهم من هرب واستجار بكم من الكفار من جملتهم اخواننا التوارق المهاجرين فى سبيل الله من ارضهم / لما ملكها الكافر واخواننا صالح بو كريم وعبد الرحيم مطارى ومسكتموهم عندكم والى الان لم تطلقوا سبيلهم وربما / بلغنا ان التوارق اخذتم عيالهم وحريمهم وهذا نقصان فى حقكم اذا انتم متصفون بالعدل والغيرة للاسلام على (. . . .)[2] / المذكورين منا ومن اخواننا وقطعنا عليكم النظر لمن هو منا ومنتسب علينا بنظر القبول والرحمة و اجارته مما / يلحقه من الظلم واخواننا محتاجون لهم فالماسول من السياده النظر فيهم بعين الرضى والرحمة وتطلقون سبيلهم / يقدمون الينا مع اول قادم والقطع على حضرتكم الا توخروهم بعد وصول هذا الكتاب بوجه من الوجوه وغيركم / يحتاج التاكيد وقصدنا عدم قطع الطريق بيننا وبينكم و اذا حصل امساك لهولاء الذين ذكرناهم فربما يودى الى / عدم ضبط الناس والحكم فيهم فلا يتوجه علينا لوم بعد ذلك ويتسع الخرق على الراقع والمومن لاخيه كالبنيان يشد / بعضه

بعضا والله تعلى يجعلنا واياكم الهادين المهديين الدلين على الخير بالتول وبالنعل
عاملين بجاه سيد / الاولين والاخرين ومنا اتم السلام وازكاه وانماه يهدى لمن حواه
المقام فى البدء والختام وصنونا / السيد محمد الرضى وكافة الاخوان يهدون للجناب
اكرم التحيه والدعوات الخيريه والسلام تاريخ ١٠ شوال / سنه / ١٢٢٠[3]

In the name of God, the Merciful, the Compassionate.

From Muḥammad Idrīs b. al-Sayyid Muḥammad al-Mahdī b. al-Sayyid Muḥammad b. `Alī b. al-Sanūsī al-Khaṭṭābī al-Ḥasanī al-Idrīsī.

To the support of the noble-minded, the flower of the eminent people of learning, scion of the noble, the benefaction of days and nights, of high ambitions and ever-increasing noble deeds, the object of the highest hope, and [ ] of soundness and perfection, the eminent sultan, son of the perfect sultan, [his] majesty Sultan `Alī Dīnār, son of Sultan Faḍl al-`Abbāsī. May God prolong his illustriousness, fulfill his hopes for the best in both worlds, and make effective his words and deeds.

After the bestowal of fragrant and unceasingly elegant salutations appropriate to [your] high station, the purpose of it is to inquire about you, and your condition. May God make it pleasant, through the sanctity of the prophet accepted [by God], may God bless him and grant him peace, honor and greatness. If you are kind enough to ask about us, all of the *ikhwān* here are well and in good health, and enjoying ample abundance. We hope to [God] Most High that you are likewise, always, through the influence of the prophet, upon whom be blessing and peace. Let it be known to your honor that for an period of a year or two God's enemy the French have directed hostilities against al-Dōr, and have driven out the inhabitants. Some of the *ikhwān* there died, while others have fled, and have sought refuge with you from the unbelievers. Among them are our brethern the Tuareg, who made the Hijra from their homeland in the path of God when the unbeliever came to rule it. These are our brethern Ṣāliḥ Bū Karīm and `Abd al-Raḥīm Maṭārī. You have detained them, and up to now you have not given them leave to go. We have heard that you may have seized the children and women of the Tuareg. This is a failing on your part, since you are known for your justice and your zeal for Islam [. . .] the above-mentioned from us and our brethern. We impress upon you to look at those who belong to us or are associated with us with an eye of approval and mercy, and of recompensation for the oppression they may have suffered. Our brethern need them. What is hoped from [your] lordship that you look at them with approval and mercy, and that you will let them go, so that they will come to us with the first person traveling. It is impressed upon [your] lordship not to delay them in any way whatsoever after the arrival of this letter. You of all people do not need to be told [this]. It is our intention that the roads between us and you not be cut, but if these whom we have mentioned are held back, that may lead to a lack of authority over the people and failure to rule them. Blame should not be directed at us hereafter. A stich in time saves nine. The believer and his brother are like a building, each part of which supports the other. May God Most High make us and you rightly-guided guides, showing the way to goodness through their words and putting it into practice through their deeds, through the exalted status of the lord of those of former and latter days [Muḥammad].

The most perfect greetings from us, and the purest and most numerous, are bestowed upon those whom your noble presence embraces at first and at last. Our twin brother al-Sayyid Muḥammad al-Riḍā and all the *ikhwān* direct toward [your] majesty the most noble salutations and benevolent prayers.

Farewell. The date is 10 Shawwāl 1330/22 September 1912.

1. Triaud, "Relations," pp. 1219-1220.

2. Lacuna, a hole was punched in the paper here.

3. The seal imprint here is not legible.

DOCUMENT 19

Document 19 seems to be a fragment of an intelligence report about northwestern affairs prepared in al-Fāshir for ʿAlī Dīnār. It is not dated, but since the mention of Italian compensation payments to the Turks seems to be a garbled reference to the Treaty of Lausanne of October 1912, it probably originated after that date. The document contained information derived from merchants recently arrived from the west, notably Ṭāhir walad Aḥmad and his associates. Ṭāhir, a Fazzānī trader of Sanūsī sympathies, had long served ʿAlī Dīnār as one of the sultan's select corps of royal merchants.[1] He had recently rediscovered his Ottoman identity as a native Libyan, however, and had made himself useful as an aide to the Turks during the short-lived Ottoman intervention in northern Chad.[2] The merchants reported that the French authorities in Chad had paid compensation for wealth taken unfairly from them by the French colonial puppet sultan of Dār Tāma.

عدد / ١ طاهر ولد احمد من جماعه غيث حضر من وداي معه عدد ٦ جمال / معه
ولد اسمه وشيه وادم من جماعة الفكي بو بكر الغدامسي ومعهم ولد يدعي /
ابراهيم حضر اجير من وداي واما خبر الجلابه النصراني كناهم من / صندوقه وصار
غريم التاماوي واهله في اموال الجلابه التي / اخذوها وتصادفوا بالمخذول حتار استلم
منهم اربعة بنادق وجملين / ظلما وعدوانا واستلم منهم واحد جواد وخمسة
وثلاثون ريال / ابو طيره ومائتان وجه جبخانه منهم ستين ابو طيره كان قصدهم /
يوصلوها لسيدنا بسلام والباقي جبخانه اسلحتهم والان احضروا معهم / سبعة
واربعون طلقه ابو طيره في تسعة تنكات وثمانيه وعشرون / ظرف فارغ / وخبر
السنوسيه مع النصاره التليان فالنصاره التزموا / بدفع ستة عشر مليون جنيه يدفعوها في

اقبال الصلح / دفعوا منها ثمانيه مليون للسنوسيه والعساكر العثمليه / وباقي عليهم ثمانية مليون يدفعوها

(Number) 1.[3] Ṭāhir walad Aḥmad from the company of Ghayth arrived from Wadai with (number) 6 camels. With him is a boy named Washīya, and Adam from the company of the Fakī Bū Bakr al-Ghadāmsī. With them is a boy called Ibrāhīm, [who] came from Wadai as an employee. As for the merchants' news: The Christian has paid them compensation out of his own treasury. The Tāmāwī and his people appropriated the merchants' wealth, which they took so that [the merchants] suffered a crippling setback. He took from them four guns and two camels in tyranny and enmity. He took from them a horse, thirty-five *Abū Ṭayra* [Maria Theresa] dollars, and two hundred rounds of ammunition of which sixty were *Abū Ṭayra*. It had been their intention to deliver these to our lord as a greeting [gift], the rest being ammunition for their [own] guns. Now they are bringing with them forty-seven rounds of *Abū Ṭayra* in nine cans, and twenty-eight empty cartridges. As for the news of the Sanūsiyya and the Italian Christians, the Christians have undertaken to pay sixteen million pounds in return for the acceptance of a truce. Out of this they have paid eight million to the Sanūsiyya and the Ottoman soldiers, and they still owe eight million [yet] to be paid.[4]

1. Triaud, "Relations," p. 1198.
2. Ciammaichella, *Libyens et Français*, pp. 159-160, 165-168.
3. The word "number" is written above the numerical figure.
4. This letter is written in eastern and not in *maghribī* script.

DOCUMENT 20

Document 20 was written in Kufra after the departure to the northern front of Aḥmad al-Sharīf in June 1912 and before the fall of `Ayn Gallaka to the French in November 1913. Muḥammad Hilāl thanked `Alī Dīnār for his generous support, and specifically for supplying the slave girls previously requested. He explained why the Sanūsī traders had been unable to dispose of some of the king's ivory. Finally, he announced the disbanding of the southern nomadic command of al-Dōr; personnel were to be transferred to the last defense of `Ayn Gallaka and livestock removed to the far north.

الحمد لله وحده / وقد ذكرت السيادة من جانب السن والريش الذى صحبة القادمين

من الطرف وان المقصود / جعلها فى سلاح وعلف وقد يسر الله من المطلوب ما

يصلكم ان شاء الله موضحا فى الكشف / الذى بيد الاخ خليل والذى بباطن جواب

السيد احمد الريفى اطلاعكم عليه فيه كفايه / وقد بقى من السن عندنا خمسة قناطير

واحدى عشرة اقه ونصف ان شاء الله اذا وجدنا / كراء سهلا نرسلها للبيع و ياتيكم

ثمنها ان شاء الله والجوارى اللتى تفضلت الحضرة / بارسالها وصلت ايضا وجاءت

على طبق المراد فالله تعلى يعلى مقامكم ويجازيكم احسن / الجزا والاخ محمد يونس

قد وقف مع الاخوان القادمين فى قضاء مصالحهم غايه الوقوف / حتى انه ترك جميع

اشغاله حتى قضوا لوازمهم جزاه الله خيرا واما الاخ غيث فانه توجه / لان بيده مالا

للناس ما امكنه التاخير وما ذكرت الحضرة من جهة الدور واهله فان / السيد احمد

الريفى ذكر لكم ما فيه الكفايه وغالب سعينا ارسلناه للجهة البحريه / والاخوان

امرناهم بالارتحال الى جهة كلك وباقى السعى ياتى الينا والمقصود راحتكم / وراحة

غيركم والنبى صلى الله عليه وسلم يقول لا يومن احدكم حتى يحب لاخيه ما يحب
لنفسه ⁄ والله تعلى يجعل المعرفة لوجهه الكريم والمحبة لذاته والله يسمعنا عنكم ما يسر ⁄⁄
ومن العبد الفقير محمد هلال ابن السيد محمد الشريف بعد اهداء وافر التحيه
واسنى التسليمات الزكيه على الحضرة ⁄ البهيه وما تفضلت به من الهديه ⁄ وصل
وبالقبول والاقبال اتصلت والله ⁄ تعلى يجازيكم باحسن الجزا انه جواد كريم ⁄
بر رحيم ⁄⁄

المقتبس النور
القدوسى احمد ابن
السيد الشريف
السنوسى
١٢٢١

Praise be to God alone.

[Your] lordship mentioned concerning the ivory and ostrich feathers brought by those coming from [your] side that the intention is to exchange them for weapons and ammunition.[1] May God facilitate [matters]. What is coming to you from [your] order, if God wills, is listed in the manifest in the possession of brother Khalīl.

As for that which is in the letter of al-Sayyid Aḥmad al-Rīfī, your examination of it is sufficient.

The remainder of the ivory here with us is five *qinṭārs* and eleven and one-half ounces. If God wills, when we can hire [camels] for it easily we will send it to be sold and send you its price, if God wills.

The slave girls whom [your] majesty was so gracious as to send us have arrived too, and they were exactly what was wanted. May God Most High elevate your station and reward you with the best of rewards.

The brother Muḥammad Yūnus greatly assisted the *ikhwān* who had come to do business, to the extent that he neglected all his own business until they took care of their needs. May God reward him well.

As for the brother Ghayth, he has set off, for he has in his possession people's wealth which does not allow for delay.

As for what [your] majesty has mentioned in regard to al-Dōr and its people, what al-Sayyid Aḥmad al-Rīfī has mentioned to you is sufficient. We have sent most of our livestock in the direction of the sea. We have ordered the *ikhwān* to move to the region of Kalaka, and the rest of the livestock will come to us. The intention is to ease [things] for you and for others. The prophet, may God bless him and grant him peace, says: "No one of you is a believer until he desires for his brother what he desires for himself."

May God Most High bestow [upon you] knowledge of His noble countenance and love for His essence. May God let us hear about you that which pleases.

From the humble servant Muḥammad Hilāl b. al-Sayyid Muḥammad al-Sharīf. After the bestowal of abundant salutations and most brilliant of pure greetings to [your] magnificent majesty, the present with which you have favored [us] arrived and has come to us with appreciation and approval. May God Most High reward you with the best of rewards, for it is a noble steed, a merciful charitable gift.

He who has acquired the Most Holy Light

Aḥmad b. al-Sayyid al-Sharīf al-Sanūsī

1321/1903-1904

1. *'Alaf* means " cartridges " or "ammunition" (Triaud, *Tchad*, p. 114). The basic meaning is "fodder"

DOCUMENT 21

Document 21 is an undated letter of appreciation to `Alī Dīnār from Muḥammad al-Shaykh Makkī b. `Abd Allāh b. Ṣāliḥ Ruz. The writer was probably a Fazzānī leader, some of whose people had sought refuge in Dār Fūr when the Italians under Miani invaded the Fazzān early in 1914.

*

بسم الله الرحمان[1] الرحيم وصلى الله على سيدنا محمد وءاله وصحبه وسلم / انه الى
سلطان المسلمين وحصن الخايفين وملاذى[1] الارامل والمساكين / وقدوة السالكين
المتمسك بسنة رسول رب العالمين المتواضع بقلبه / وقلابه فى جميع حركاته وسكناته
لمالك يوم الدين وظلا ظليلا وملجا لجميع / المسلمين نصره الله واعانه على رفع منار
الدين بجاه سيد الاولين والاخرين / صلى الله عليه وعلى ءاله وصحبه فى كل لمحة
ونفس عدد ما وسع علم الله / ءامين سلطان زمانه وفريد عصره السلطان على دينار
ابن السلطان زكرياء / ادام الله عزه ونصره وايده على جميع اعدايه اعانه واعلاه ءامين
السلام / عليكم ورحمته وبركاته ومغفرته ومرضاته وازكى تحياته وان تفضلتم عنا /
بالسؤال فانا ولله الحمد بمدد سادتنا رضى الله عنهم وارضاهم بخير / عميم وربح
جسيم والحمد لله انما سالتم عن الطليان ظهروا من جميع الاماكن / اطرابلس [2]
وبنغازى وهم فى حد الرز يتعلوا فى البحر من جميع الاماكن والوطن / لعيث ابن
السنوسى لله الحمد ويذكروا فى ارض السودان عن قريب / ياتوا الى زاويت ترو والحمد
لله قدموا ناسكم واخبروا على انكم ريحتم / ناس رز وكرمتموهم بالكسوه والهنا
وريحتموهم غاية الراحه اتانا منهم / جواب يثنوا عليكم بالخير جزاكم الله عنا وعن

جميع احسن الجزا ونحن ان / ان[3] شاء الله ان تدموا اسيادنا الى الجهه القبليه
نكون معهم وانت الحمد / لله الذى الفتح بينك وبين اسيادنا فى هذا الزمان الدرب
بالامان والعز والنصر / والله يطول عمركم فى رضاء الله ءامين والسلام فى البدء
والختام / من خديمكم محمد الشيخ مكى / بن عبد الله بن صالح رز

In the name of God, the Merciful, the Compassionate. May God bless our lord Muḥammad, his family and companions, and grant them peace.

To the sultan of the Muslims, a fortress for the fearful and a refuge to the widowers and to the poor, an example to those who follow the holy path, he who holds fast to the *sunna* of the messenger of the Lord of the Universe, humble in heart and soul in all his doings toward the Master of the Day of Doom, a protecting shade and sanctuary for all the Muslims, may God grant him victory, aid him in raising the minaret of religion through the exalted status of the lord of those of former and latter days, may God bless him, his family and companions in every glance and breath, as many as God's wisdom accommodates. Amen. [To] the sultan of his time and peerless one of his age, Sultan `Alī Dīnār, son of Sultan Zakariyā'. May God prolong his power and [endow him] with victory and support him, and aid him against and elevate him above all his enemies. Amen. Peace be upon you, and His mercy and blessings, forgiveness, acceptance, and purest salutations.

Should you favor us by asking [about us], praise be to God, through the support of our masters, may God be pleased with them and please them, we are [in a condition of] comprehensive wellbeing and vast gain, God be praised. If you ask about the Italians, they have arisen from all places, [from] Tripoli and Benghazi, and are at the border of al-Ruz.[4] They are coming up out of the sea from every place and nation to destroy Ibn al-Sanūsī. Praise be to God. They say that soon in the land of the Sudan they will come to the *zāwīya* of Qirū. Praise be to God, your people arrived and told [us] that you had relieved the people of Ruz and had been generous to them with clothing, and [other] useful things, and that you had relieved them completely. A letter from them came to us in which they spoke well of you. May God reward you well for our sake, and for the sake of all.

If God wills, when our masters go to the south we will be with them; and you, praise be to God, are the one who has opened with power, support and protection a road between yourself and our masters in these times. May God lengthen your life in His favor. Amen. Peace at the beginning and the end.

From your servant Muḥammad al-Shaykh Makkī b. `Abd Allāh b. Ṣāliḥ Ruz.

1. Spelled as shown.

2. We omit *alif, lām, alif* before Aṭrābulus, an apparent scribal error or a false beginning.

3. Dittography in original.

4. The precise geographical location of Ruz or al-Ruz is unknown to us.

DOCUMENT 22

Document 22 was written in Kufra on 20 November 1914 by `Abd al-Raḥīm Maṭārī, erstwhile associate of Ṣāliḥ Abū Karīm. The two leaders had been arrested in 1912 during `Alī Dīnār's crackdown upon the nomadic raiders of al-Dōr, then released at the request of the Sanūsī leaders (Document 18) and expelled from Dār Fūr early in 1913. It had then been their misfortune to fall prey to the French attack of 15 May upon their caravan on the road to Gouro.[1] It would seem that the French soon released `Abd al-Raḥīm, along with the ambassador Abū Bakr al-Ghadāmsī and other survivors of the attack against whom they held no specific grievance. Through the present letter `Abd al-Raḥīm sought to reestablish good relations with `Alī Dīnār and to obtain permission to return to Dār Fūr. To that end he put down in writing some of the political gossip that would perhaps ordinarily have been conveyed orally. He included not only an account of his own far-flung misadventures since his brush with the French, but also an account of the First World War in Libya as he understood it.

بسم الله الرحمن الرحيم / انه الى حضرة السلالة الطاهره والعبادة الظاهره وامير
المومنين وسلطان المسلمين سيدنا ومولانا السلطان علي دينار بن سيدنا ومولانا /
المرحوم السلطان زكريا بن السلطان محمد الفضل ادام الله ملكه ووجوده وبلغه من
خير الدارين متصوده اما بعد مزيد السلام عليكم و (. . .)[2] / فليكون فى شريف
علمكم ان سئلتم عن اخبار طرفنا السيد محمد عابد وصل ارض النززين وحين التريخ
فى الشياطى ووصل كونس (التليانى)[3] / الى طرف صيف النصر [4] ومراده صيف
النصر يبقى من اتباعه وحين ما اتى اليه كونس تحارب هو واياه ووقعى [4] بينهم

اربعة (عشر)[3] / نفر ستت من صيف النصر وثمانيه من كونس وانكسر مدفع كونس
وكل احد شرع على صينه[4] وحين ما بلغ الخبر الى / السيد صفى الدين رسل
اعيال صيف النصر الذى معاه وسيدى محمد صالح ولد سيدي محمد البكر بلى
الصلح بين كونس وصيف / النصر ولا حين التاريخ ما اتانا خبر الصلح وان دولة
الطليان ضهرت[4] من اعمالت اطرابلس كلها ما عاد تفوا انفيت /[3] فى اطرابلس نفسه
وان شاء الله يخرجوا منها وتتريح العباد وان جيهت بنى غازى متوجه اليها السيد
ادريس / ولا حين التريخ موصل اليها ودولت الطليان ما زالت في المرامر كلها الا مرمر
الزويتين ظهروا منه والسيد احمد / الشريف مستلم هو ومحمد رشاد ودولت
الامانيه ومرادهم احرابت الانقليز ولا حين التريخ ما صار بينهم حرب / فى السابق
سيوه تبع الانقليز وحين التاريخ تبع السيد احمد حط فيها نقطه فى اجل الجمرك
ستين نفر واخذ من اهلها / خمسين نفر عملهم عسكر تحته في السلوم وصارت سيوه
من جملت اتباعه وان شاء الله سبحانه وتعلى يات بما فيه الخير / ويعجل الفرح
للمسلمين بجاه سيد الاولين والاخرين وان سئلت عن حالنا مان[4] مسكني عنكم الا جبر
علينا من قلت / الرزق في الاول مان[4] اسجر الا فى اجل امانه فى الحاج حسن بابل
الهوصاتى بطرف سيد احمد الريف وهي على (يده)[3] / من اصلها وبعد وفات
سيدى احمد الريف استلمه السيد احمد الشريف وحين ما اتيت له قال ما نعطيه لك
ومنعه عني / وانا ما فى يدي الا شيء قليل توجهت الى مصر ومراد بالقدوم اليكم
على درب النهود والتنتوف الذى في يدي / عملته فى شاه ورسلته الى الابيض فى
البابور ومراد بصفر[4] معاه ومنعتنى دولت الانقليز من الركوب في البابور / والشاه
فات فيه ومشتر في البابور وانا بتيت فى مصر حتى اتوا جماعه منا وتوجهت الى

الكنره وحين التريخ مقيم / بها حتى يفتح الله لنا باب من ابوابه وحين ما نلتوا بشى
نقدروا على الطريق ما عندنا الا الله وانتم نقدم اليكم / اذا لقينا رزق والا ما لقينا لا
بد ثم لا بد من قدومنا الى طرفكم ما عندنا راحه الا وطنكم ولا تنسانا من الفاتحه
والدعاء / الصالح وان طالبين منكم وحشاكم من التقصير وانت ما تتورى وغيرك
محتاج التكيد [4] ولا بد من غير مامور عليكم ترسلوا / لنا جواب صحبت ابننا محمد
ابو محجوب نتبركوا به ويطمئن خواطرنا به ودمتم بخير ودائى لكم الخيرات
وسعادة الاوقات / بتريخ شهر الله محرم يوم ٢ سنه ١٣٣٢ من غلامكم الحقير عبد
الرحيم ابن الحاج صالح ابو مطاري

In the name of God, the Merciful, the Compassionate.

To the presence of the one of pure descent and of manifest devotion, commander of the faithful and sultan of the Muslims, our lord and master Sultan `Alī Dīnār, son of our lord and master the late Sultan Zakariyā, son of Sultan Muḥammad al-Faḍl. May God prolong his rule and his presence, and make him attain his wishes for the best in both worlds.

Thereafter: Abundant greetings to you and [ ]. Let it be known to your noble honor that if you ask about news from our side, Sayyid Muḥammad `Ābid has arrived in the land of the Fazāzīn [the Fazzān], and is now in al-Shiyāṭī. Kūnus the Italian came to the area of Sayf al-Naṣr with the intention of making Sayf al-Naṣr one of his followers. When Kūnus reached him, they fought each other. Between them there fell fourteen souls, six of Sayf al-Naṣr and eight of Kūnus. Kūnus's cannon broke and everyone drew his sword. As soon as the news reached Sīdī Ṣafī al-Dīn, he sent the children of Sayf al-Naṣr who were with him, and Sīdī Muḥammad Ṣāliḥ, son of Sīdī Muḥammad al-Bakr to test the truce between Kūnus and Sayf al-Naṣr, but to date no news of this truce has come to us. The Italian Empire has emerged in all the districts of Tripoli, except ( )[5] in Tripoli itself. God willing, they will withdraw from it so that the worshipers will find rest. As for the area of Benghazi, Sayyid

Idrīs has gone there. To date he has arrived there. The Italian Empire is still in all the Marmarica, even in the [region] of the two *zāwiyas*.[6] Sayyid Aḥmad al-Sharīf has taken over (command); he and Muḥammad Rashād and the German Empire intend to fight the English, but to date there has been no warfare between them. Formerly Sīwa followed the English, but now it follows Sayyid Aḥmad. He put a customs post of sixty people in it. He took fifty of its people and made them soldiers under him at al-Salūm, and Sīwa has joined the ranks of his followers. If God Most High wills, praise be to Him, he will bring success and hasten the joy of the Muslims through the exalted status of the lord of those of former and latter days.

If you ask about our condition, we were only kept away from you because we were constrained by the shortage of provisions in the first place. I was only urged on because of the consignment with al-Ḥājj Ḥasan Bābal al-Hūṣātī who is with Sayyid Aḥmad al-Rīfī. Originally it was in [Ḥasan's] possession, and Sīdī Aḥmad al-Sharīf received it after the death of Sīdī Aḥmad al-Rīfī. But when I went to him, he said: "We won't give it to you," and he denied it to me. I had nothing in hand, except for a very little. I went to Egypt in the hope of coming to you by the road through al-Nahūd. The little in my possession I converted into sheep and sent them to El Obeid by steamboat in the hope of traveling with them. The English Empire forbade me to board the steamboat, but the sheep left with it, being sold on the steamboat. I stayed in Egypt until a group of us gathered; then I went to Kufra. These days I am residing there, until God opens one of His gates for us. When we find something, we will be ready for the road, but we have nothing but God and you. We will come to you if we find provisions, and [even] if we do not, we must, we must come to your country. Only your country can give us relief. Do not forget us in the *fātiḥa* and in pious prayers, even if we take a long time. God forbid that you disappoint us. Do not conceal yourself from us, for you of all people do not need to be told, and you will definitely, without instructions, send us via our son Muḥammad Abū Maḥjūb a letter in which we find blessing and which puts our minds at ease. May you remain well, and may well-being and happiness draw close to you. On the date of God's month of Muḥarram, the second day of it, in the year 1333/20 November 1914. From your lowly and humble servant `Abd al-Raḥīm b. al-Ḥājj Ṣāliḥ Abū Maṭārī.

1. Triaud, "Relations," pp. 1219-1220.
2. Lacuna.
3. Lacuna, conjectural reading.
4. Spelled as shown.
5. The meaning of these two words is unclear.
6. "The two *zāwiyas*:" the exact geographical reference is unclear.

DOCUMENT 23

Document 23 is the first of seven letters considered here that focus upon `Alī Dīnār's attempt to collect the large shipment of ammunition his ivory had purchased in Kufra (Documents 15, 16, 20) but which had never been delivered to Dār Fūr. Document 23, in its present form dated only to the year 1333/1914-1915, is known only through an imperfect English translation. In it `Alī Dīnār attempted to reopen contact with Aḥmad al-Sharīf after an interval of hiatus; the head of the Sanūsiyya had left Kufra in the middle of 1912 to take personal command at the Mediterranean front, leaving Kufra to the oversight of Muḥammad `Ābid--in whom `Alī Dīnār no longer had complete confidence. In his letter `Alī Dīnār indicated that he had sent to Kufra a shipment of camels, some as a gift to the brotherhood and others as transport home for his previously-purchased ammunition. It is possible that the original of this letter was delivered to Kufra by `Alī Dīnār's envoy Aḥmad, former *`aqīd al-Zabāda* of Wadai; if so, it should be more precisely dated to about July 1915. At that time the Anglo-Egyptian authorities in Khartoum were sparing no effort to infiltrate the court of Dār Fūr preparatory to invading the kingdom, and it is not implausible that one of their spies might have obtained access to state correspondence. It is not known whether or not the letter in fact reached Aḥmad al-Sharīf.

The usual complimentary titles etc.[1]

To El Sayed Ahmed El Sherif Ibn El Sayed Mohammed El Sherif El Senusi,

After the usual greetings etc. and enquiring about you and your state of affairs, I am quite well and hope you are enjoying good health.

It is a long time since we received any news from you which we believe is due to pressure of work in the cause of the Jehad for the sake of God, and such being your intentions, they are worthy of praise. May God give you prosperity to do what is good in His sight.

We are sending you with our servant Ahmed thirty camels as a present to help you in your cause and which we hope you will accept. Our servant Ahmed has also been detailed to purchase firearms and ammunition and has been given some camels for sale. Kindly send the articles you have for us on deposit, for the transport of with Ahmed has been provided with the necessary camels. Please hand them over to Ahmed with a message from you and when Ahmed has completed his duty, send him back to us at once. The Medjidia[2] dollars have practically ceased to exist and the only coins in circulation at present are the Khurda[3] piasters, otherwise we would have sent cash in payment of what he has got to buy from your country.

We are also sending you two Ardebs[4] of wheat.

In conclusion please accept our greetings and salutations.

1333 (1915).

1. Of this document only a free and condensed English translation is available. It was most probably prepared by a Sudanese or Egyptian translator of the Intelligence department (NRO Intelligence 5/3/40: Papers Concerning Ali Dinar. Folder 2: Letters from Senussite Personalities to Ali Dinar.

2. See glossary under *Majīdī* dollar.

3. The *khurda* (literally, "scrap metal") piaster is probably the "Girsh Radeina" described by H.A. MacMichael in his "Notes on Darfur, Wadai, Dar Sula, etc., 1916 (NRO Intelligence 5/3/39): "This represents Ali Dinar's highest effort at debasing the coinage. The "Radeina" is a very thin, roughly circular scrap of copper, the size of a shilling, with a blurred inscription to the effect that it was struck at Fasher. It is made for the most part out of kitchen utensils." The name "Radeina" meant "we have accepted it." According to MacMichael, people had been reluctant to accept it, but had been compelled to do so. The name was therefore "a jocular allusion to the baseness of the currency and the necessity of making the best of it."

4. See glossary under *ardabb*.

DOCUMENT 24

Document 24 is a letter of 8 April 1915 in which the Majābra merchants resident in Kufra attempted to disassociate themselves from the policies of Muḥammad `Ābid. At a time when relations between the sultan and the Sanūsī commander in Kufra were strained, it was significant that the ethnic communities of northern merchants (see also Documents 25 and 28) took the initiative in opening their own direct correspondence with Dār Fūr over the heads of the Sanūsī leaders. They thanked `Alī Dīnār for opening the new eastern road from Dār Fūr to Kufra via Merga.

بسم الله الرحمن الرحيم وصل[1] الله على سيدنا محمد وعلى ءاله وصحبه وسلم / انه

الى سيدنا السيد السلطان على دينار نصره الله واعزه واهلك عدوه واذله / ءامين

السلام الاتم ورضوانه الاعم عليكم سيدنا ورحمة الله وبركاته ومغفرته / ومرضاته

وبعد ثان تفضلتم بالسئال عنا وعن كافت جملتنا الحمد لله بخير وعافيه ونعمة /

متوالي ضافيه ما نسئل الا عنكم وعن تجارة ارضكم وحكمكم وعدلكم ءامين هاذا /

وسابتا بلغنا مرسولكم من درب مرقه ففرحنا بذالك الدرب لاجل (فتحه)[2] / من الله

واسباب منكم مبرك ان شاء الله عليكم وعلينا وتباشرنا به واقصوين[3] / غايت السرور

الله يزيد عدلكم ويوفقتكم لما يحبه ويرضاه ءامين وان / شاء الله بعد هاذا الوقت

كافت التجار اذا لقوا اسلحه يتونكم به / وسلامنا يشمل كافت التجار الذى بطرنكم

ومن هو منكم واليكم ولا تنسونا / بصالح اعمالكم فى خلواتكم وجلواتكم وعلى الله

التبول انه اكرم مسئول وخير / مامول ودمتم ودامت معاليكم وتنورت بالعز

والنصر ايامكم ولياليكم ءامين / والسلام عليكم ورحمة الله تعالى وبركاته فى كل

لحة ونفس عدد ما واسعه ، علم الله والسلام بتاريخ ٢٢ جماد اول عام ١٢٢٢ ،

كافت المجابره القيمين بالكفره

In the name of God, the Merciful, the Compassionate. May God bless our lord Muḥammad, his family and companions, and grant them peace.

To our lord Sultan `Alī Dīnār. May God grant him victory and power and destroy and abase his enemy. Amen. The most perfect greetings and His most comprehensive acceptance be upon you, our lord, and the mercy of God, His blessing, His forgiveness, and His favor.

Thereafter: If you should kindly inquire about us and our whole community, praise be to God we are well and in good health, [enjoying] unceasingly abundant prosperity. We ask only about you, about the commerce of your land, your government, and your justice. Amen. Some time ago your messenger reached us via the Merga road. We rejoiced at that road, whose opening was from God by means of you. If God wills, it will be a blessing for you and us. We rejoiced at it, reaching the utmost limit of joy. May God increase your justice and make you succeed in that which He loves and that of which He approves. Amen. If God wills, henceforth all merchants, whenever they find weapons, will bring them to you. Our greeting includes all the merchants who are with you, or travel from, or to, you. Do not forget us in your prayers both private and public. Acceptance is up to God, for He is the Most Generous Answerer of Requests and the Most Benevolent Fulfiller of Hopes. May you and your nobles endure. May your days and nights be illuminated with might and victory. Amen. Peace be upon you, and the mercy of God Most High, and His blessings, in every glance and breath, as many as God's wisdom accommodates. Farewell. On the date of 23 Jumāda I in the year 1333/8 April 1915. All the Majābra residing in Kufra.

[1]Spelled as shown.

[2]Lacuna, conjectural reading.

[3]Conjectural reading.

DOCUMENT 25

Document 25 was written in Kufra on 8 April 1915 for a number of presumably notable residents who were probably traders, and who definitely sympathized with `Alī Dīnār's special emissary Ghayth Bū Karīm in his difficulties with Muḥammad `Ābid. Ghayth had arrived in Kufra in November 1914 to collect the store of `Alī Dīnār's ammunition, which at that moment Muḥammad `Ābid was engaged in discharging at Miani and the Italian occupiers of the Fazzān. Ghayth was kept waiting throughout the winter of Sanūsī victories; his resources were exhausted and he became dependent upon the charity of his hosts, who wrote to the king on his behalf.

بسم الله الرحمن الرحيم وصلى الله على سيدنا محمد وبه نستعين واتوكل الله ينصر
سلطان المسلمين السيد علي دينار ءامين / الى امير المومنين سيدنا السيد السلطان علي
دينار بن سيدنا السيد السلطان زكرياء بن سيدنا السيد / السلطان فضل ايده الله
بالنصر والظفر ءامين السلام عليكم سيدى ورحمة الله تعلى وبركاته وازكى تحياته /
ومغفرته ومرضاته وبعد فالامر المهم والمقصد الاعظم هو السوال عنكم وعن كلية
احوالكم اعزكم الله / ونصركم الى يوم القيمه ورقاكم كل درجة عليه وكملكم
باحسانه ءامين هذا سيدى اتانا اخونا الشيخ غيث / ءاخر فتوح شهر الله محرم
ففرحو به كافة اهل البلد غايه واسروا به نهاية فلما وصل دلا [1] على محل سيدى /
السيد محمد عابد واعطاه مكاتيبكم الكرام وقام فى ضيافته تلك الايام وشاوره على
الخصم الذى بينه / وبين عيلت ابو حليته وجميع حقوقه اللازمات له والذى لسيده
قال له السيد محمد عابد المذكور قيم / عند ناسك حتى نعديك بجميع اللازم لك

ولسيدك السلطان المنصور قال له نعم اتانا واقام بمحلنا / حتى اكل جميع الذى بيده
من كثرة المقامه وبعد ذالك كتبنا له جواب على ان مرسول سيدنا جميع / ما عنده من
ابل وغيره باعهن واكلهن مصروف وحين الوقت المطلوب من فضلكم تعديه لسيده /
السلطان بما امكن رد لنا رقيمته بخط يده على انه يصبر ونسفروه بما يريد بعد ذالك
صبر صبرا / كثيرا حتى بلغ اربعة اشهر سمع الاخ المذكور سيدى محمد يبغى السفر
لناحيت الغرب بعد ذالك مشا / للسيد المذكور بنفسه وتابله وخاطبه وقال السيد
محمد عابد ما نسافر حتى نعديك بالذى تريده / وترضى سيدنا السيد السلطان علي
دينار ما زال يرتجي حتى السيد محمد العابد سافر وتوجه للغرب على / نية الجهاد
هاذه مادت الاخ المذكور فها هو متوجه لكم ان شاء الله يصلكم بالسلامه الله ينصرك /
ويعون حكمك ءامين ويا سيدنا فرحنا بالدرب الذى فتحتوه بامر من الله ومنكم غاية
الفرح والسرور / وان شاء الله ما ينتطعو عنكم التجار طرفة عين لاجل الناس كلها
تريد داركم وحكمكم غير هذا / الوقت من فضلكم واعدال حكمكم تاخرنا لاجل
الارض حاميه ان شاء الله على هذا البرد وياتونكم ناس / كثيره والسلام عليكم
ورحمه الله تعلى وبركاته فى كل لمحة ونفس عدد ما وسعه علم الله والسلام بتاريخ
٢٢ جماد الاول / سنه / ١٢٢٢ / من خداديم خدامكم / الشيخ حمد / التذاني
/ الشيخ عمر / بو عبد السيد / الشيخ محمد بو بدر / الشيخ بدر بو يونس[2] /
الشيخ محمد بو عبد الله / الشيخ مفتاح / بو كزيم / وكافة من يحتو عليهم من
الرجال

In the name of God, the Merciful, the Compassionate. May God bless our lord Muḥammad. Him we ask for help, and in Him I trust. May God grant victory to the sultan of the Muslims, the lord `Alī Dīnār. Amen.

To the commander of the faithful, our lord Sultan `Alī Dīnār, son of our lord Sultan Zakariyā', son of our lord Sultan Faḍl. May God support him with victory and triumph. Amen. Peace be upon you, my lord, and the mercy of God Most High, and His blessing, His purest salutations, His forgiveness, and His favor.

Thereafter: The matter of great importance and the object of greatest significance is to inquire about you and all your affairs. May God give you power and victory until the Day of Reckoning, elevate you to every high rank, and make you perfect through His beneficence. Amen.

Furthermore, my lord, our brother Shaykh Ghayth came to us late on the first day of God's month of Muḥarram. All the people of the land were extremely happy and very pleased. When he arrived, he was taken to the place of my lord al-Sayyid Muḥammad `Ābid, gave him your noble letters, and remained those days as his guest. He discussed with him the dispute between him and the family of Abū Ḥalayqa and all the rights properly his and those of his lord. The said Sayyid Muḥammad `Ābid said to him: "Stay with your people until we send you back with all you and your lord the victorious sultan need." He [Ghayth] said to him: "Very well." He came to us and stayed at our place until he had eaten everything he had because of the length of the waiting. After that we [the authors of the present letter] wrote to him [Muḥammad `Ābid] a letter, to the effect that the envoy of our lord [Ghayth, envoy of `Alī Dīnār] had sold and consumed for his maintenance all he had in the way of camels and the like. "At this time, what is asked of your grace," [they wrote to Muḥammad `Ābid], is to send him back to his lord the sultan with whatever is possible." He [Muḥammad `Ābid] replied to us with a letter in his own handwriting that he [Ghayth] should be patient, and [the reply continued], "we shall send him off with what he wants." After that he was very patient, until four months had passed. Then he heard that the said brother Sīdī Muḥammad wanted to travel in the direction of the west. Upon that, he went to the said Sayyid in person and met him and talked with him. Sayyid Muḥammad `Ābid said: "We will not travel until we have sent you back with all that you want and what pleases our lord Sultan `Alī Dīnār."

He [Ghayth] continued to have hope until Sayyid Muḥammad `Ābid traveled, and set out toward the west for the purpose of the *jihād.* This upset the said brother greatly. Now he is coming to you [`Alī Dīnār]. If God wills, he will arrive safely. May God give you victory and aid your rule. Amen.

O my lord, we rejoiced with the greatest joy and pleasure at the road which you opened by God's command and yours. If God wills the merchants will not be cut off from you even for a moment, for all the people desire your country and your rule--not only at this [difficult] time--because of your generosity and the justice of your rule. We have been delayed because the land has been in fury but, in the light of this [recent] calm [the opening of the road], many people will be coming to you. Peace be upon you, and the mercy of God Most High, and His blessing, with every glance and breath for as many as God's wisdom accommodates. Farewell. On the date of 23 Jumāda I in the year 1333/8 April 1915.

From the servants of your servant, Shaykh Ḥammad al-Qadhāfī, Shaykh `Umar b. `Abd al-Sayyid, Shaykh Muḥammad Bū Badr, Shaykh Badr Bū Yūnus, Shaykh Muḥammad Bū `Abd Allāh, Shaykh Muftāḥ Bū Karīm, and all the men who are associated with them.

1. Spelled as shown.

2. The two seal imprints that follow the names are not legible.

DOCUMENT 26

Document 26 was written in Kufra on 10 April 1915 by `Alī Dīnār's special envoy Ghayth Bū Karīm. He explained that although he had reached Kufra safely some time before, he had failed to accomplish his mission. Muḥammad `Ābid had seized the store of `Alī Dīnār's ammunition in Kufra and had ridden west to expel the Italians from the Fazzān. The sultan's emissary had exhausted his resources and had been obliged to borrow from his hosts at Kufra, some of whom were responsible for sending Document 25 to the king on his behalf.

بسم الله الرحمن الرحيم وصلى الله على سيدنا محمد / الى سيدنا ومولانا سيدى

السلطان امير المومنين علي دينار بن سيدى السلطان زكرياء بن سيدى السلطان /

فضل فضله الله واعزه واعطاه الظفر والنصر واجمله ءامين السلام عليكم سيدى

ورحمة الله تعلى وبركاته / وازكى تحياته ومغفرته ومرضاته وبعد الامر المهم

والمقصد الاعظم هو اجتماعنا فى محلاتكم والنظر لكم / والرضى منكم واحوالكم يبلغ

ذالك المولى ءامين هذا وقد توجهنا منكم سابقا على احسن حال / واوصلنا الكفر

بخير وعافيه واتينا للسيد محمد واعطيناه مكاتبيه واخبرناه بما كان وما يكون

وقال / لنا نعم بما قلتم وما لنا زياده فى قضاء حوايج سيدكم لاكن توجه امكث عند

ناسك واصبر حتى نطلبوك / مكثنا عند ناسنا كما قال حتى بلغنا اربعة اشهر ويكون

فى شرفكم ان محل الكفر الصرف فيها تعيب [1] / الجمل ما يصرف جمعه واحده

الحاصل لاجل حوايجنا قمنا ذالك المقام المذكور وبعدها سمعنا انه / مسافر لناحيت

الغرب محلات فزازين وواد حرير وغيرها مشينا له وخاطباه [1] شفاها بكل شيء /

قال لنا ان شاء الله نسافروا جميعا انت تتوجه لسيدك وهو يغرب فى طلب الجهاد

ومشا وما واجبنا / حتى بكلام وها نحن قايمين فى الكفر منتظرين لكرامة سيدنا
السلطان المذكور على ما يامرنا نقيموا / او نتوجهوا لسيدى احمد والسيد ادريس
باذن منكم وجوابات او ناتوكم فى فور ونخبروكم ان / امانتنا توجه سيدى محمد
معه منها عشرة ءالاف زرف [1] لاجل سابقا مخزون عند الحاج على قرجيله / المجبرى
وشردوه وشالوه معهم وانتم اسياد الامر والتدبير والعبد ما له الا ما يقوى / له
سيده وان سالتم سيدى عن حالنا ما فى يدنا شىء كله الذى فى يدنا صرفناه
وحين التاريخ / نتدينو من الناس وناكلو وسيدى محمد ما اعاننا ولو بمد غله والا
راس سكر وحضرت سعادتكم / ما يخفى عليها شىء وها هى تبلغكم بندقه طليانيه
بياض الورقه معها ثمانين وجه الا واحد / وان شاء الله محمد وبو بكر ياتوكم
بالسلامه والمطلوب من فضلكم ياتونا عاجلا لا يتعطلو عنا وان / سالتم عن كافة
الاخبار سيدنا يخبروكم القادمون عليكم شفاها والامر لله ولكم سيدى والسلام
بتاريخ / ٢٥ جماد الاول / سنه / ١٣٢٢ / عبدكم غيث بو كريم / الزوى

In the name of God, the Merciful, the Compassionate.

May God bless our lord Muḥammad.

To our lord and master, my lord the sultan, commander of the faithful, `Alī Dīnār, son of my lord Sultan Zakariyā', son of my lord Sultan Faḍl.

May God give him preference and power, bestow upon him triumph and victory, and treat him well. Amen. Peace be upon you, my lord, and the mercy of God Most High, and His blessing, His purest salutations, His forgiveness, and His favor.

Thereafter: The matter of great importance and the goal of greatest significance is to be united with you where you are, to see you, and to find pleasure in you and your condition. May Our Master bring that about. Amen. Some time ago we left you in the best condition. We reached Kufra safely and in good health. We came to Sayyid Muḥammad and gave him his letters.

We told him everything, past and present, and he said "yes" to what you said. [He said:] "We do not have any surplus from which to meet your lordship's needs, so go stay with your own people and be patient until we ask for you." We stayed with our own people, as he said, until we had spent four months. Let it be [known] to your honor that making payments in this place Kufra is difficult; one is not [even] paid for a camel on one Friday. The upshot was, that for the sake of our needs we left the said place. Then we heard that he [Sīdī Muḥammad ʿĀbid] was traveling toward the west, to the places of Fazāzīn,[2] Wādī Ḥarīr,[3] and elsewhere. We went to him and told him everything orally. He said to us: "If God wills we will all travel--you to your lord," while he would go west in search of the *jihād*. He left, having laid no obligation upon us, even of words. Here we are, staying in Kufra, awaiting the generosity of our lord the said sultan. According to what he orders us to do we will stay, or go to Sīdī Aḥmad and al-Sayyid Idrīs with your permission and with letters, or come to you in [Dār] Fūr. We inform you that Sīdī Muḥammad has taken with him our consignment, including 10,000 cartridges. These were formerly in storage with al-Ḥājj ʿAlī Qarjayla al-Majabrī, but they drove him away and carried the [cartridges] off with them. You are the master of command and supervision, for the slave has no power save what his master gives him. My lord, if you ask about our condition, in our hand there is nothing, for all that was in our hand we have paid out. As of now we are incurring debts with people in order to eat. Sīdī Muḥammad has not helped us, not even with a *midd* of grain or a head of sugar, but from the presence of your majesty nothing is concealed. There is coming to you an Italian gun, white of plate, and with it eighty rounds, less one. If God wills, Muḥammad and Bū Bakr[4] will come to you safely. It is requested from your generosity that they will come to us quickly; may they not be delayed from [coming back to] us. Our lord, if you ask about all the news, those arriving will inform you orally. It is for God to command, and for you, my master. Farewell. On the date 25 Jumāda I in the year 1333/10 April 1915. Your servant, Ghayth Bū Karīm al-Zuwayyī.

1. Spelled as shown.
2. Probably a reference to the Fazzān or the inhabitants of the Fazzān.
3. Wādī Ḥarīr's exact geographical location is not known to us.
4. Possibly Muḥammad Yūnus and Bū Bakr al-Ghadāmsī.

DOCUMENT 27

In response to the failure of the mission of Ghayth Bū Karīm ʿAlī Dīnār sent an armed official expedition to Kufra under the command of Aḥmad, formerly Dūd Murra's *ʿaqīd al-Zabāda*, to collect what the Sanūsī leaders owed him. Document 27, available only in flawed English translation, is Muḥammad ʿĀbid's long-delayed response to the missions of Ghayth Bū Karīm and the *ʿaqīd* Aḥmad. If the version extant is true to the original, Muḥammad ʿĀbid avoided the question of his debt to ʿAlī Dīnār by stressing Sanūsī victories in the war. Ghayth the first debt-collector was sent packing with a rifle and twenty rounds as a present to the king, while the expedition of the *ʿaqīd* Aḥmad was mentioned only as having lost heavily in transit. This was not the sort of answer that would have pleased ʿAlī Dīnār, and it is not surprising that under these circumstances he would have attempted (Document 23) to reach Aḥmad al-Sharīf over the head of Muḥammad ʿĀbid.

From Mohammed El Sherif Abed El Senussi to Sultan Ali Dinar.[1]

Dated 27th Higga 1333, 5.11.1915.

Greetings and very flattering salutations. I beg to inform your honoured person that the Sayids and all who are here are well. We are merry that your messengers have arrived and they told us that your honour is very well, for which we thank God. They stayed several days with us, but all the Sayids had been absent. The father[2] who had been the last one to leave for Tripoli, will by the help of God, drive away the accursed from Tripoli and other places. When the Italians, enemies of God, first came to Tripoli our Head the Sultan[3] encountered them and helped them in every possible way. Then the Grand Sayid Ahmed El Sherif our uncle, took up the undertaking to fight them, and he destroyed them. In the meanwhile the "Daula" (Turkish Empire[4]) and Germany fought them at sea. Sayid Ahmed continued to fight them for a time and when joined by El Sayid Mod. Safai El Din, he annihilated them. The Grand Sayid, leaving Sayid Safai El Din in the West, proceeded to the Egyptian frontier. Sayid Safai El Din captured many Italians and returned to Jedabi.[5] The father Sayid went to Tripoli and is now besieging it. May God grant predominance to Islam.

Re the present which you sent to the Sayids, much of it was lost on the journey and what arrived here was distributed to those concerned respectively - may God reward you with the best reward.

Sheikh Gheis and his company are proceeding to you - They are taking to you a rifle with 20 rounds as a small present which we pray you will accept. Your letter has been sent to the father with a letter from us. We hope that you will be quite satisfied and that you will treat us as a father and as before and favour us with your continual communication.

1. See Doc. 23, note 1.
2. "The father" and "the father Sayid" probably refer to Aḥmad al-Sharīf al-Sanūsī.
3. The Ottoman Sultan Muḥammad Rashād.
4. Turkish Empire: "Ottoman" would be more correct.
5. Jedabi: Jadhabiyya was the Sanūsī headquarters south of Benghazi.

DOCUMENT 28

Document 28 of 7 November 1915 was prepared by the Zuwayya merchant community of Kufra to disassociate themselves from the policies of Muḥammad `Ābid and to respond favorably to `Alī Dīnār's renewed initiative. It is comparable in intent to Document 24, prepared by the Majābra community in Kufra. In both cases Muḥammad `Ābid's refusal to deliver `Alī Dīnār's ammunition, however justified from the Sanūsī commander's tactical perspective, alienated not only the Dār Fūr sultan, but also the corps of Libyan private merchants who depended upon the sultan's good graces for the quiet pursuit of their own fortunes.

بسم الله الرحمن الرحيم وبه نستعين واتوكل عليه واصلي واسلم على سيدنا محمد
سيدى[1] الاولين والاخرين / الى سيدنا السلطان سيدى [1] العرب والعجم والاماكن
والبلدان سيدنا السلطان علي دينار ابن السلطان زكرياء ابن السلطان محمد الفضل /
ابن السلطان عبد الرحمان الرشيد ابن السلطان بكر ءايده الله بالنصر ورفع قدره
واتم الفخر ءامين السلام عليكم ورحمة الله تعلى / وبركاته ومغفرته ومرضاته وبعد
الامر المهم والمقصد الاعظم هو السوال عنكم وعن كلية احوالكم السنيه لا زلتم فى نصر
/ وظفر وفخم مرضيه هذا سيدنا قد تشرفنا بمنظومكم وكل ما شرحتم فيه فهمناه
وحمدنا الله سبحانه وتعلى على عزكم / وشكرناه واتانا العقيد ومن معه من عساكر
دولتكم على احسن حال ومكثو بطرفنا لتضاء الازم[1] والاستعمال وها هم / قادمون
لسعادتكم ان شاء الله ياتوكم بالسلامة وحسن المثال ومعهم اخواننا غيث وبعض انفار
للتجاره والذى / فى ناحيت برقه والسلوم ان شاء الله على اثرهم يقدمو لطرفكم بنية

التجاره لاجل محلكم ما فيه الا الربح خاطي من الخساره ⁄ وكافة ازويه مسرورين بمكاتيبكم ومراسيلكم وفتحت الدرب على بلدكم نعسى تتابلهم بعين الرضى وقضاء لوازمهم ⁄ وحسن الدعا مع بلوغ سلامنا لخدامكم المتربين والانجال المكرمين ومن عندنا كافة الكبير والصغير ⁄ بالنصر داعيين ودمتم ودامت معاليكم وتنورت بالعز والنصر ايامكم ولياليكم ءامين والسلام بتاريخ ءاخر ذى الحجه ⁄ سنه ٢٢(١٢)[2]

⁄ كافة مشايخ ازويه الذين هم عيلت الشيخ غيث ⁄ بو كريم منهم عشره محفضيه[1] لتقلتك ⁄ وعشره باسم التجاره والمحفضين المذكورين ⁄ كبيرهم محمد ريف بن عبد الكريم لفرج

In the name of God, the Merciful, the Compassionate. Him we ask for help. I trust in him, and invoke His blessings and peace upon our lord Muḥammad, the lord of those of former and latter days. To our lord the sultan, lord of the Arabs and non-Arabs, of the localities and the lands, our lord Sultan `Alī Dīnār, son of Sultan Zakariyā', son of Sultan `Abd al-Raḥmān al-Rashīd, son of Sultan Bukr. May God support him with victory, elevate his rank, and perfect [his] glory. Amen. Peace be upon you, and the mercy of God Most High, and His blessings, His forgiveness, and His favor.

Thereafter: The most important matter and the most significant objective is to inquire about you and all your legitimate affairs. May you not cease to enjoy victory, triumph, and grandeur gratifying to God. Our lord, we were honored by your poetic composition, and we have understood all that you have set forth in it. We gave praise and thanks to God Most High, glory be to Him, for your power. The *`aqīd* and the soldiers of your government who accompanied him have come to us in the best condition. They resided with us to transact the necessary business. They are now coming to Your Majesty; if God wills, they will come safely and with good counsel, and with them will come our brethern, Ghayth and some individuals to trade. If God wills, those who are in the district of Barka and Salūm will come immediately after them; they are coming to you with the intention of trading, for your place has nothing in it but profit that allows recovery from loss. All the Zuwayya are delighted at your letters and missives. You opened the road to your country. Will you not receive them favorably and take care of their requirements? The best of prayers with the conveyance of our greetings to your closest servants and the noble princes. Here all, great and small, are praying for victory. May you and your high nobility endure, and may your days and nights be illuminated with power and victory.

Amen. Farewell.

On the date of the last day of Dhu'l-Ḥijja in the year 1333 / 7 November 1915.

Of all the shaykhs of the Zuwayya who are of the family of Shaykh Ghayth Bū Karīm ten are to guard your caravan and ten for the purpose of trade. The commander of the said guards is Muḥammad Rīf b. ʿAbd al-Karīm Lafraj.

1. Spelled as shown.

2. Lacuna, conjectural reading.

DOCUMENT 29

Document 29 was written on 18 December at Jabal Mīrū outside al-Fāshir, announcing the return to Dār Fūr of the emissary Ghayth Bū Karīm and a party of northern merchants. According to Anglo-Egyptian spies, who were watching this caravan closely, the *`aqīd* Aḥmad had also accompanied the party from Kufra; the expedition had lost so many camels in transit that the party was threatened with death by thirst, and had to be rescued by a relief column from al-Fāshir. The *`aqīd*'s surviving forces had accompanied the returning relief column directly to the capital, while Ghayth and the merchants followed more slowly, and by this letter observed the customary protocol of approach to the royal city.

بسم الله الرحمن الرحيم / الى الاجل الافضل الاغز الامثل غاية الامال ونهاية المجد
والكمال/ سيدنا سيدى على دينار سيدنا سيدى السلطان على دينار ابن السلطان /
زكريا ابن السلطان محمد الفضل ابن السلطان عبد الرحمان الرشيد ابن / السلطان بكر
ايده الله بالرضي والرضوان وختم له بالسعادة و (الرضي)[1] / والرضوان السلام
عليكم ورحمة الله تعلى وبركاته ومغفرته و (مرضاته)[1] / وازكى تحياته ورضوانه
هذا فان سالتم عنا وعن كافة الجهديه الذى / مع العقيد احمد وصلوا على احسن بحالة
الصحة والعافيه وربنا ينضر[2] / ينضرنا وجهكم على خير بجاه النبي الشفيع صل[3] الله
عليه وسلم فان / سلتم[3] سيدى على الغزان الذى اتوا معنا الجمله عشرون نفر زويه
ومن / الاخوان اخوا السيد بو بكر الجمله اثنين وعشرون فان سالتم/ عن اسيادنا
الذى بالكفره كلهم فى ناحية البحر سوى سيدى محمد / الشريف وسيدى احمد بو
سيف خال سيدى السيد محمد ادريس / وكافة الاخوان الذى بالكفره والزوية

والمجابره كلهم فرحانين ⁄ مضمئنين [3] على فتح الطريق وربنا ينصركم ويفرج على
كافة المسلمين ⁄ بوجودكم ءامين والعشرون نفر منهم عشره تجار بيدهم مقدار (. . .)
⁄[4] بندقه وعشره انفار اتوا معنا محافضين [3] على الجبخانه الذى لكم ⁄ والحمد
لله وصلنا الى جبل ميروا على احسن حال ودمتم ودامت ⁄ لكم السعاده ولكم
الحسنى وزياده والسلام بتاريخ صفر الخير ⁄ ١٠ ⁄ من عبدكم غيث بوا كريم

In the name of God, the Merciful, the Compassionate.

To the most illustrious, excellent, mighty exemplar, highest of [our] hopes, epitome of glory and perfection, our lord, Sīdī `Alī Dīnār, our lord, Sīdī Sultan `Alī Dīnār, son of Sultan Zakariyā, son of Sultan Muḥammad al-Faḍl, son of Sultan `Abd al-Raḥmān al-Rashīd, son of Sultan Bukr. May God support him with good will and approval and place upon him the seal of happiness, good will and approval. Peace be upon you, and the mercy and blessings of God Most High, and His forgiveness and approval, and the purest of His salutations, and His approval.

If you ask about us, and about all the slave soldiers [*jihādiyya*] who are with the *`aqīd* Aḥmad, they arrived well, in a state of health and good condition. May Our Lord, for our sake, make your countenance shine for the good, through the influence of the interceding prophet, may God bless him and grant him peace. If you, my lord, ask about the Fazzān who came with us, the group consists of twenty souls of the Zuwayya, and of the *ikhwān*, the brother al-Sayyid Bū Bakr [and myself], the total [thus] consisting of twenty-two [persons]. If you ask about our *sīdīs* at Kufra, all of them are [away] in the vicinity of the sea except for Sīdī Muḥammad al-Sharīf and Sīdī Aḥmad Bū Sayf, maternal uncle to Sīdī al-Sayyid Muḥammad Idrīs. All the brethern who are in Kufra, and the Zuwayya and the Majābra, are delighted and relieved at the opening of the road. May Our Lord give you victory and give relief to all the Muslims through your presence. Amen. Of the twenty persons, ten are merchants bearing a quantity of . . .[5] guns; ten are people who came with us to guard the ammunition which is for you. Praise be to God, we have reached Jabal Mīrū[6] in the best of conditions.

May you endure; may happiness endure for you, and a happy outcome, and more than that. Farewell. On the date of 10 Ṣafar *al-Khayr*[7] [1334 / 18 December 1915]. From your servant Ghayth Bū Karīm.

1. Lacuna, conjectural reading.
2. Dittography.
3. Spelled as shown.
4. Lacuna, *khā'* and *mīm* are visible.
5. The number is only partly readible, but must be five or a multiple of five.
6. The exact geographical location of Jabal Mīrū is unknown to us.
7. *Al-Khayr*: a common epithet of the month of Ṣafar.

DOCUMENT 30

The final letter of the present collection survives only in English translation, apparently gathered by Anglo-Egyptian spies from within `Alī Dīnār's chancery during the early weeks of 1916; at that time the Condominium authorities were sparing no effort to organize the impending conquest of Dār Fūr. `Alī Dīnār wrote again to Aḥmad al-Sharīf, congratulating him on the recent series of Sanūsī victories and alerting him to the probability of an imminent break between his own government and the authorities in Khartoum. He also protested the conduct of Muḥammad `Ābid in regard to the undelivered ammunition. If the original letter of which this is a translation was in fact delivered to Aḥmad al-Sharīf it could not have reached him much before the Anglo-Egyptian invasion of Dār Fūr.

After the usual titles etc.

To El Sayed Ahmed El Sherif Ibn El Sayed El Sherif Mohammed El Senusi.

After usual greetings:

I beg to enquire about you and about all your affairs. I am all right and hope you are in perfect health. Please note that Gheis Abu Karim arrived here a couple of days ago and told us about your high reputation and your efforts towards religion and praised you highly. I have been pleased to hear of your endeavours to exalt the word of God and your "Jehad" against the enemies of God in the name of God, in order to attain his blessings and good will. May God bless you and reward you on behalf of Islam and may he also recompense you. I pray God to help you and grant you victory over the enemies of God. May he disappoint them and confound them and torture them through your hands and uphold the word of truth and faith and destroy the heathens and idolators.

We have been moved by the religious zeal and fervant faith to rise by the power and might of God for the protection of the religion of God against the enemies of God, the infidels and opposers of Mohammedan laws, who are neighbouring us in the Sudan. We shall shortly proclaim the Jehad for the sake of God and you shall hear how the enemies of God will suffer hardships and fetters at our hands.

We pray God to grant you and us the victory he promised in his holy book where he said: "And we shall grant victory with the believers."

Your brother (or son) in-law Mohammed El Abed has behaved very badly whilst we were busy in the case of Christians. We have asked him to send us the ammunition deposited with him but he refused to do so and our messengers returned without it.

The Mohammedans in Eastern Sudan, who are under the British rule, have all embraced Christianity and forsaken Islam. Their notables have written asking us to follow the Christian faith intending to lead us astray but we have not listened to them. Their letters and misleading articles published in the newspapers in which they praise the British Government are sent herewith for your perusal.

In conclusion accept our greetings and best salams.

23 rd Rabi' I 1334

27.1.1916

(True copy)[1]

1. See Doc. 23, note 1.

SELECT BIBLIOGRAPHY

PRIMARY SOURCES:

NATIONAL RECORDS OFFICE, KHARTOUM

Intelligence 2/3/1	Ali Dinar Historical.
Intelligence 2/3/14	Ali Dinar Historical.
Intelligence 2/15/125	Notes on the History of Senussism and its relations to the African possessions of European Powers. Part I, 1822-1902 (Major G.T. Forestier-Walker); Part II, 1902-1905 (Captain R.C.R. Owen).
Intelligence 5/3/40	Papers concerning Ali Dinar. Folder 2: Letters from Senussite Personalities to Ali Dinar.
Darfur 1/13/16	Occupation of Darfur: Senussi Activities & Western Frontier Posts.
Darfur 1/14/18	Army / Occupation of Darfur: Intelligence Reports, from H.A. MacMichael, 1915-1916.
Darfur 1/14/19	Army / Occupation of Darfur: Correspondence with Ali Dinar, 1915-1916.
Darfur 1/33/170	Events on the Western Frontier, 1899-1910.

SECONDARY SOURCES

Aḥmad Ṣidqī al-Dajjānī. *Al-Ḥaraka al-Sanūsiyya Nashā'atuhā wa-Numūwuhā fi'l-Qarn al-tāsi` `ashr.* Beirut: Dār Lubnān, 1967.

Ali, A. Yusuf. *The Holy Qur'an: Text, Translation and Commentary.* Brentwood, Maryland: Amana Corp., 1983.

Amery, H.F.S. *English-Arabic Vocabulary for the use of officials in the Anglo-Egyptian Sudan.* Cairo: Al-Mokattam Printing Office, 1905.

Asad, Talal. *The Kababish Arabs: Power, Authority and Consent in a Nomadic Tribe.* New York: Praeger, 1970.

Atiyah, Samuel Bey. "Senin and Ali Dinar," *Sudan Notes and Records*, VII, 2 (1924), 63-69.

`Awn al-Sharīf Qāsim. *Al-Lahja al-`Āmmiyya fi'l-Sūdān.* Khartoum: Al-Dār al-Sūdāniyya li'l-Kutub, 1972.

Baier, Steven. "Trans-Saharan Trade and the Sahel: Damergu, 1870-1930," *Journal of African History*, XVIII, 1 (1977), 37-60.

Beehler, Commodore W.H. *The History of the Italian-Turkish War, September 29, 1911 to October 18, 1912.* Annapolis: US Naval Institute, 1913.

Beeston, A.F.L., T.M. Johnstone, R.B. Serjeant and G.R. Smith, eds. *Arabic Literature to the End of the Umayyad Period.* Cambridge: Cambridge University Press, 1983.

Bollati, Ambrogio. *Enciclopedia dei nostri Combattimenti Coloniali Fino al 2 Ottobre 1935-XIII.* Torino: Giulio Einaudi, 1936-XIIII.

Cachia, Anthony. *Libya under the Second Ottoman Occupation (1835-1911).* Tripoli: Government Press, 1945.

Childs, Timothy. *Italo-Turkish Diplomacy and the War over Libya, 1911-1912.* Leiden: Brill, 1990.

Ciammaichella, Glauco. *Libyens et Français au Tchad (1897-1914): La Confrérie senoussie et le commerce transsaharien.* Paris: CNRS, 1987.

Ciasca, Raffaele. *Storia Coloniale dell'Italia Contemporanea.* Milan: Ulrico Hoepli, 1938-XVI.

Cordell, Dennis. "Eastern Libya, Wadai and the Sanūsiya: A Ṭarīqa and a Trade Route." *Journal of African History*, XVIII, 1 (1977), 21-36.

De Vecchi, Paolo. *Italy's Civilizing Mission in Africa.* New York: Brentano, 1912.

Dozy, R.P.A. *Supplément aux Dictionnaires Arabes.* 2 vols. Beirut: Librairie du Liban, 1968.

Dozy, R.P.A. *Dictionnaire Détaillé des Noms des Vêtements chex les Arabes.* Beirut: Librairie du Liban, n.d.

Evans-Pritchard, E.E. *The Sanusi of Cyrenaica.* Oxford: Clarendon, 1949.

Feraud, L. Charles. *Annales Tripolitaines.* Tunis: Tournirs, 1927.

Forbes, Rosita. *The Secret of the Sahara: Kufara.* New York: Doran, 1921.

Franconie, Marc, ed. *Karl Moritz von Beurmann: Voyages et explorations 1860-1863.* St.-Illide: Gibanel, 1973.

Haimann, Giuseppe. Cirenaica (Tripolitania). 2nd ed. Milano: Ulrico Hoepli, 1886.

Hassanein Bey, A.M. *The Lost Oases.* New York: Century, 1925.

Hillelson, S. *Sudan Arabic English-Arabic Vocabulary.* London: Sudan Government, 1925.

Holt, P.M. *The Mahdist State in the Sudan, 1881-1898.* 2nd ed. Oxford: Clarendon, 1970.

Houtsma, M.Th. *et al. The Encyclopaedia of Islam.* Leiden: Brill, 1934.

Joos, C.D. "Le Ouadai, le Dar el Kouti et la Senoussia en 1904: Matériaux pour étude de l'histoire des États d'Afrique Centrale," *Études Camerounaises*, No. 53-54 (octobre-décembre, 1956), 3-17.

Kapteijns, Lidwien. "The Organization of Exchange in Precolonial Western Sudan," in Leif O. Manger, ed. *Trade and Traders in the Sudan* (Bergen: University of Bergen, 1984), pp. 49-80.

Kapteijns, Lidwien. *Mahdist Faith and Sudanic Tradition: A History of the Masālīt Sultanate, 1870-1930.* London: Routledge and Kegan Paul, 1985.

Kapteijns, Lidwien and Jay Spaulding. *Een Kennismaking met de Afrikaanse Geschiedenis.* Muiderberg: Coutinho, 1985.

Kapteijns, Lidwien and Jay Spaulding. "Precolonial Trade Between States in the Eastern Sudan, c.1700 - c.1900." In Norman O'Neill and Jay O'Brien, eds. *Economy and Class in Sudan* (Aldershot: Avebury, 1988), pp. 60-89.

Kapteijns, Lidwien and Jay Spaulding. *After the Millennium: Diplomatic Correspondence from Wadai and Dār Fūr on the Eve of Colonial Conquest, 1885-1916.* East Lansing: African Studies Center, Michigan State University, 1988.

Kapteijns, Lidwien and Jay Spaulding, "Gifts Worthy of Kings: An Episode in Dār Fūr - Taqali Relations," *Sudanic Africa* 1 (1990), 61-70.

Khadduri, Majid. *Modern Libya: A Struggle in Political Development.* Baltimore: Johns Hopkins, 1963.

Klopfer, Helmut. *Aspekte der Bewegung des Muḥammad Ben `Alī as-Sanūsī.* Wiesbaden: Otto Harrassowitz, 1967.

Lapworth, Charles. *Tripoli and Young Italy.* London: Swift, 1912.

LaRue, G.M. "'Terrible Droughts Followed by Famines:' Towards an Appreciation of the Role of Drought in the History of Dar Fur, ca. 1750-1916." Unpublished Paper, Presented at the Annual Meetings of the African Studies Association, Los Angeles, 25-28 October, 1984.

Le Gall, Michel. "The Ottoman Government and the Sanusiyya: A Reappraisal." *International Journal of Middle Eastern Studies*, XXI, 1 (1989), 91-106.

Mohammed ben Otsmane el-Hachaichi. *Voyage au Pays des Senoussia à travers La Tripolitaine et les Pays Touareg*. Paris: Challamel, 1903.

Nachtigal, Gustav. *Sahara and Sudan IV: Wadai and Darfur*. Trans. Allan G.B. Fisher and Humphrey J. Fisher. Berkeley: University of California Press, 1971.

Nachtigal, Gustav. *Sahara and Sudan II: Kawar, Bornu, Kanem, Borku, Ennedi*. Trans. Allan G.B. Fisher and Humphrey J. Fisher. London: Hurst, 1980.

O'Fahey, R.S. *Enigmatic Saint: Aḥmad Ibn Idris and the Idrisi Tradition*. London: Hurst and Company, 1990.

O'Fahey, R.S. and M.I. Abū Salīm. *Land in Dār Fūr: Charters and related documents from the Dār Fūr sultanate*. Cambridge: Cambridge University Press, 1983.

Pankhurst, Richard and Douglas H. Johnson. "The great drought and famine of 1888-92 in northeast Africa." In Douglas H. Johnson and David M. Anderson, eds. *The Ecology of Survival: Case Studies from Northeast African History* (Boulder: Westview, 1988), pp. 47-70.

Reissner, Johannes. "Die Idrīsiden in ʿAsīr. Ein historischer Überblick," *Die Welt des Islams* XXI (1981), 164-192.

Rossi, Ettori. *Storia di Tripoli e della Tripolitania*. Roma: Istituto per l'Oriente, 1968.

Said, Edward W. *Orientalism*. New York: Random House, 1978.

Spaulding, Jay. "The Management of Exchange in Sinnār, c. 1700." In Leif Manger, ed. *Trade and Traders in the Sudan*. (Bergen: University of Bergen, 1984), pp. 25-48.

Spaulding, Jay. *The Heroic Age in Sinnār*. East Lansing: African Studies Center, Michigan State University, 1985.

El-Tayib, D. Griselda. "Women's Dress in the Northern Sudan." In Susan Kenyon, ed. *The Sudanese Woman* (London: Ithaca Press, 1987), pp. 40-66.

Theobald, A.B. *ʿAlī Dīnār, Last Sultan of Darfur, 1898-1916*. London: Longmans, 1965.

Triaud, Jean-Louis. *Tchad 1900-1902: Une Guerre Franco-Libyenne Oubliée? Une confrérie musulmane, la Sanūsiyya face à la France*. Paris: Harmattan, 1987.

Trimingham, J. Spencer. *Sudan Colloquial Arabic*. 2nd ed. London: Oxford University Press, 1946.

Tubiana, Marie-José and Joseph Tubiana. *The Zaghawa from an Ecological Perspective*. Rotterdam: A.A. Balkema, 1977.

Wright, John. *Libya, Chad and the Central Sahara*. Totowa: Barnes & Noble, 1989.

Waal, Alexander de. *Famine that Kills: Darfur, Sudan, 1984-1985*. Oxford: Clarendon, 1989.

Wehr, Hans. *A Dictionary of Modern Written Arabic*. Wiesbaden: Otto Harrassowitz, 1971.

Ziadeh, Nicola A. *Sanūsīyah: A Study of a Revivalist Movement in Islam*. Reprinted with an appendix by R.J.I. Ter Laan. Leiden: Brill, 1983.

Zulfo, ʿIsmat Hasan. *Karari: The Sudanese Account of the Battle of Omdurman*. Trans. Peter Clark. London: Frederick Warne, 1980.

GLOSSARY

Abū Ṭayra dollar	Maria Theresa dollar.
Abū Ṭayra gun	A type of gun.
'aqīd	A common (military) title of administrative officials in Wadai.
ardabb	A dry measure of 198 liters.
Dār al-Islām	Lands ruled by Muslim rulers.
dirham	A generic term for silver coins, in these documents either the Maria Theresa dollars or the *Majīdī* dollar.
fātiḥa	The opening verse of the Qur'ān.
'Īd al-fiṭr	The Feast of Fastbreaking, one of the major Islamic holidays which ends the month of Ramaḍān.
jihād	Holy war (against unbelievers).
ikhwān	Literally "brethren," full members of the Sanūsī brotherhood.
khalīfa	successor, vicar.
Majīdī dollar	A silver Ottoman coin worth one-fifth of a Turkish gold pound, or twenty piasters. It was introduced by Sultan `Abd al-Majīd (1839-1861).
midd or *mudd*	A standard grain measure of varying size.
qinṭār	Unit of weight. An Egyptian *qinṭār* of the early twentieth century weighed 44,928 kg; the contemporary *qinṭār* of Tripoli weighed 51,282 kg.
Sayyid	In this context the title given to any male descendant of the Grand Sanūsī, Muḥammad b. `Alī.
Sīdī	Title of respect most commonly applied to the *Sayyids* and their close associates.
sunna	The example, in word and deed, of the Prophet.
'ulamā'	Muslim learned or holy men.
Ustādh	"Teacher," often used as a title of respect.
zāwiya	Sanūsī lodge or headquarters.

INDEX OF NAMES